# Compiere 3

An essential and concise guide to understanding and implementing Compiere

**Andries L Pretorius**

[PACKT] open source *
PUBLISHING    community experience distilled

BIRMINGHAM - MUMBAI

# Compiere 3

First published: June 2010

Production Reference: 1220610

Published by Packt Publishing Ltd.
32 Lincoln Road
Olton
Birmingham, B27 6PA, UK.

ISBN 978-1-849510-84-4

www.packtpub.com

Cover Image by Faiz Fattohi (faizfattohi@gmail.com)

# Credits

**Author**
Andries L Pretorius

**Reviewer**
Yves Sandfort

**Acquisition Editor**
Steven Wilding

**Development Editor**
Wilson D'Souza

**Technical Editor**
Pallavi Kachare

**Indexer**
Hemangini Bari

**Editorial Team Leader**
Akshara Aware

**Project Team Leader**
Priya Mukherji

**Project Coordinator**
Prasad Rai

**Proofreaders**
Dirk Manuel
Chris Smith

**Production Coordinator**
Melwyn D'sa

**Cover Work**
Melwyn D'sa

# About the author

**Andries L Pretorius**, CA(SA) ACMA(UK), an accountant by training who understands programming, is founder of Astidian Systems a leading Compiere and professional open source applications development and consulting house, which is a pioneer in deploying Compiere within its market for more than the last seven years.

He has led many Compiere implementations as well as SAP R/3 and Great Plains (now MS Dynamics) implementations both from a consulting and business owner perspective. He has been the lead architect in many custom Compiere enhancements and has over 15 years of experience in ERP and CRM applications.

His experience includes CFO and COO of leading South African retail, wholesale, and distribution enterprises, financial manager at a telecoms provider in Singapore as well as being articled at Deloitte Johannesburg and New York offices.

You can reach him on his blog on www.astidian.com/blog.

To my wife Erika and family who had the patience for endless weekends of stolen time.

Thanks to Jorg and Kathy for architecting the next generation ERP, Ashley G Ramdass, Neil Gordon, Steven Wilding for his patience, Prasad Rai and Wilson D'Souza at Packt Publishing.

# About the reviewer

**Yves Sandfort** is a veteran in the Internet business and a well known and respected commercial open source evangelist. He combines in-depth technical knowledge with the ability to quickly adopt real business demand. Especially his good understanding of national and international financial relations and how to build, maintain and successfully rollout financial solutions (CRM/ERP/BI) make him an expert you don't want to miss on your project.

Yves Sandfort has implemented commercial open source applications like Compiere, Pentaho or SugarCRM in companies of all sizes around the world (Europe, USA, Hong Kong, Australia). The comdivision group, which he founded in 1996, is proud partner of many commercial open source projects and shows that there is the possibility of commercial success in the open source industry.

I would like to thank some open source veterans and investors like Andre Boisvert, Larry Augustin, and Jorg Janke who always supported my work and helped me to build a successful business around the open source ecosystem. Without these people I would not be in the position to work around the globe and review books like this one.

# Table of Contents

# Preface

In its simplest form a business entity is the legal or otherwise manifestation of the entrepreneurial spirit of human beings. Information is required in order to record, control, analyze, and predict the entrepreneurial process. Information systems supporting these activities have greatly evolved in the last 40 years from the very basic to the very complex. By its very nature information systems have been required to constantly change to keep up with the entrepreneurial spirit. **ERP (Enterprise Resource Planning)** systems as they have come to be known evolved from the eventual requirement to have an integrated system across the entire business process (end to end).

Celebrating and maturing from an open source project to a leading edge competitor in the ERP space, Compiere offers best-of-class functionality on a model-driven architecture, the latest enterprise platform-independent web technologies (GWT, Java, JBoss, Oracle / Postgress), while maintaining open standards, value, flexibility, scalability, and most of all an integrated ERP platform that can be extended with ease.

Compiere is widely regarded as the top Open Source ERP and its name was derived from the Italian word for **to fulfill / deliver**.

In this book we will introduce you to understanding Compiere functionality by exploring the different essential business processes. We will cover the setup, the processes of Sales, Purchasing, Inventory, and Financial Management as well as the advanced aspects like Workflow, project planning, and migration.

Every chapter is illustrated by example so as to facilitate quick, concise, and practical reading. The book's aim is to take your basic knowledge of the ERP environment and ensure that you gain a practical understanding of the critical functional aspects during the process of evaluating or implementing Compiere.

# What this book covers

Chapter 1, *Evaluating the Compiere System* aims to highlight to the reader aspects related to evaluating the Compiere ERP system as well as the differences in product editions.

Chapter 2, *The Initial Compiere Setup* introduces Compiere terminology as well as initial setup of the organizations, account elements, documents, and users.

Chapter 3, *Customers and Sales Process* deals with the aspects of setting up your customers and detailing the sales process from Sales Order to Invoicing.

Chapter 4, *Product and Material Management* explains the concepts of a products, price lists, and discount schemas. It also illustrates concepts of Material Management, which controls the aspects of quantity through standard warehousing control.

Chapter 5, *Procurement Management* covers Procurement Management with regards to the processes from Request for Quotation, through Purchase Orders, Invoicing, and Material Receipt, to the Payment of vendors.

Chapter 6, *Compiere Financial Management...* aims to explain the accounting and financial aspects of the system as in the end businesses must rely on accounting information.

Chapter 7, *Advanced Aspects* covers an overview of the Application Dictionary (AD) as well as examples of creating custom fields and setting up a basic document workflow.

Chapter 8, *Project Planning for Go-live and Beyond* highlights the aspects related to project planning from people, functional, and technical points of view. We will also relate aspects regarding post-go live and migration.

# What you need for this book

For this book you will need a basic understanding of accounting and ERP systems. The Compiere Evaluation software can be downloaded from: http://www.compiere.com/wstore (contact support@compiere.com for an evaluation license) or the Community Editions are available from http://sourceforge.net/projects/compiere/files/ (the latest being version 3.3). Installation instructions (Windows or Linux) are included in the download but can also be obtained from http://www.compiere.com/support/installation.php. Wiki support is available from http://wiki.compiere.com. The required databases can be obtained from either Oracle.com (Oracle 11*g*) or Enterprisedb.com (EDB 8.3R2). The required Sun Java Development Kit (JDK version) can be obtained from http://java.sun.com/javase/downloads/index.jsp (update 5 or later).

# Who this book is for

If you are considering Compiere or want to easily implement Compiere in your organization, this book is for you. This book will also be beneficial to system users and administrators who wish to implement an ERP system. No previous knowledge of Compiere is required.

# Conventions

In this book, you will find a number of styles of text that distinguish between different kinds of information. Here are some examples of these styles, and an explanation of their meaning.

Code words in text are shown as follows: "It is found under your main installation directory as `c:\Compiere2\RUN_setup.bat` (Windows) or `/home/Compiere2/RUN_setup.sh` (Linux):".

**New terms** and **important words** are shown in bold. Words that you see on the screen, in menus or dialog boxes for example, appear in the text like this: "Select the **Initial Tenant Setup** from the menu and enter your tenant details as follows:".

# Reader feedback

Feedback from our readers is always welcome. Let us know what you think about this book—what you liked or may have disliked. Reader feedback is important for us to develop titles that you really get the most out of.

To send us general feedback, simply send an e-mail to `feedback@packtpub.com`, and mention the book title via the subject of your message.

If there is a book that you need and would like to see us publish, please send us a note in the **SUGGEST A TITLE** form on `www.packtpub.com` or e-mail `suggest@packtpub.com`.

If there is a topic that you have expertise in and you are interested in either writing or contributing to a book, see our author guide on `www.packtpub.com/authors`.

# Customer support

Now that you are the proud owner of a Packt book, we have a number of things to help you to get the most from your purchase.

# Errata

Although we have taken every care to ensure the accuracy of our content, mistakes do happen. If you find a mistake in one of our books—maybe a mistake in the text or the code—we would be grateful if you would report this to us. By doing so, you can save other readers from frustration and help us improve subsequent versions of this book. If you find any errata, please report them by visiting http://www.packtpub.com/support, selecting your book, clicking on the **let us know** link, and entering the details of your errata. Once your errata are verified, your submission will be accepted and the errata will be uploaded on our website, or added to any list of existing errata, under the Errata section of that title. Any existing errata can be viewed by selecting your title from http://www.packtpub.com/support.

# Piracy

Piracy of copyright material on the Internet is an ongoing problem across all media. At Packt, we take the protection of our copyright and licenses very seriously. If you come across any illegal copies of our works, in any form, on the Internet, please provide us with the location address or website name immediately so that we can pursue a remedy.

Please contact us at copyright@packtpub.com with a link to the suspected pirated material.

We appreciate your help in protecting our authors, and our ability to bring you valuable content.

# Questions

You can contact us at questions@packtpub.com if you are having a problem with any aspect of the book, and we will do our best to address it.

# 1
# Evaluating the Compiere System

Managing an integrated business that requires an ERP system is a challenge in itself, so the defining question when one starts to look at an ERP system is: will an ERP add value to the business and be worth the investment? ERP systems costs money, they require new skills, they require employees and business to adapt, and, ultimately, they take a lot of management time to implement.

Most notably, an ERP system has the purpose of providing management with an integrated information and transaction processing environment. This will provide the required financial and non-financial data and information for insightful reports that inform and underwrite decision making. Information systems must measure the effective and optimum use of enterprise resources, whether they are defined as people, products, services, or assets.

This chapter deals with assisting you in evaluating the Compiere system. In this chapter we shall:

- Give you a list of the core functionalities of the Compiere system
- Indicate which critical decision factors you must use in evaluating the system
- Present an understanding of the different Compiere product editions
- Show you where to get more information on Compiere

# When do you look at Compiere

The Compiere system is certainly suitable in the following organizational circumstances:

| Circumstance | Compiere advantage |
|---|---|
| **Outgrowing existing system** | |
| The business is outgrowing its existing systems. Generally, the business was doing fine on a small accounting package, but now requires additional functionality. It may also require a more scalable enterprise database, or the number of users and the complexity of the business is expanding. | Compiere's technology stack offers a growing company the enterprise scalability platform required. Functionality and transactions volumes can be scaled based on specific user needs. |
| **Existing system is old technology** | |
| The existing system is so old that support cannot be easily obtained and the technology is just hanging by a thread. This is usually the case with long-standing or older generation management. For example, a family business that has been in existence for many years and the legacy system has just always worked, but finally a decision has to be made as to a new system. | Compiere offers the current Java and web technology platform , which is based on open architecture and standards, throughout its offering. |
| **Dynamic system requirement** | |
| More progressive and dynamic management where the underlying technology is as important to the business as the business itself. | Due to its open source nature, Compiere offers a flexible and transparent technology platform. |
| **Value proposition** | |
| Large businesses that are evaluating ERP vendor systems and are analyzing the costs versus return. | Compiere provides a competitive licensing model up to large-scale Enterprise levels. |

# Compiere's core ERP functionality

In differentiating the Compiere product offering from the traditional ERP offering, Compiere is known for its **multi's**:

- Multi-language for Documents and User Interface
- Multi-currency for transacting in or reporting in foreign currencies
- Multi-tax, supporting different tax systems (Sales, VAT, and combinations)
- Multi-costing in parallel (for example, Standard Costing, Average, and Lifo)
- Multi-accounting for legal reporting using different accounting principles (selecting Cash, Accrual, or International GAAP principles)
- Multi-Tenant and Multi-Organization for different branches, and legal entities, reporting and dimensional structures

The Compiere Core Functionality includes a rich dynamic business functionality framework, and we shall cover some of these aspects in detail in later chapters.

# Compiere system administration

System administration functions are the normal administrator functions that you would expect in a system. These functions include:

- **User administration**: Manages the users that can log on to the system, password management, date control, and user preferences.
- **Role management**: What users can do in the system, who can access which windows and processes, and ultimately what users can see into the system.
- **Tenant setup**: Managing the detail of the main legal entities, departments, cost centers, and sales regions.
- **Document settings**: Document formats, document types, and document sequences.
- **System utilities**: Back-up and restore of critical system settings, although mostly this is handled through external database scripts.
- **System settings and parameters**: Includes database location, licensing, user defined control parameters, and formats.
- **Functional settings**: Set-up includes Tax, currencies, units of measure, and payment terms.
- **The Compiere Application Dictionary (AD)**: The application dictionary refers to meta-data in the application that determines the context and behavior of windows and data elements across all aspects of the Compiere application. For the non-programmer, this meta-driven model greatly reduces application core program-level customization requirements, and also gives system administrators the power to interact on a business logic point of view.

# Sales cycle to accounts receivable

Typical sales cycle functionality includes:

- Preparing quotations and sales orders
- Sales order to customer invoicing
- Sales order to delivery (shipment to customer)
- Batch invoicing and printing
- Preparing purchase orders from sales orders
- Payment receipts at the time of ordering or invoicing

# Purchasing cycle to accounts payable

Typical purchasing cycle functionality includes:

- Preparing requisitions and purchase orders
- Purchase order to vendor invoicing
- Purchase order to material receiving
- Vendor invoicing (including expense creditors)
- Processing payments to suppliers

# Business partner management

Business partners include customers, vendors, and employees. Typical functionalities include:

- Creating and editing business partners
- Classifying and grouping business partners
- Creating locations, contacts, and banking information
- Credit limit management
- Allocating different types of discount schemas to business partners

# Financial Accounting Management

Typical functionalities include:

- Setting up and maintaining multiple accounting schemas and currencies
- Creating, editing, and grouping account elements, and general ledger management
- Posting actual and budget entries to accounts through journal entries
- Running financial reports, trial balances, and accounts details
- Account at various activity and low-level cost detail

# Cash management

Typical functionalities of cash management include:

- Allocating payments and receipts to accounts receivable / accounts payable orders or invoices
- Processing cash journal entries
- Managing, correcting, and viewing historic allocations
- Open item reporting and aging
- Accounting for actual bank statement transactions
- Reconciling system entries to the bank statement
- Dunning (statement) processing

# Customer Relationship Management

Typical functionalities of CRM management include:

- Capturing leads and sales opportunities
- Opportunity reporting
- Converting leads to business partners
- Processing requests to action for sales representatives

# Inventory and material management

Products are anything in the system that you can purchase or sell and that has a price. Typical functionalities of material management include:

- Creating and editing of product and service items
- Grouping of products
- Managing product pricing and discount schemas
- Transactional listing reporting
- Serializing of products (lot control)
- Creating additional product attributes (size, length)
- Costing products to warehouse locations
- Accounting for various costing methods (standard, average, and LIFO)
- Inventory moves, adjustments, valuations, and write-offs
- Auto generation of replenishment orders

# Light Production

Typically functionalities of light production include:

- Defining and editing Bills of Materials
- Creating or editing kits
- Processing production work orders

# Integrated advanced ERP functionality

Due to its open source nature, all modules or components of Compiere are seamlessly integrated and are available separately or as part of the entire offering:

| Advanced Functionality | Description |
| --- | --- |
| Request Management | Services Request Management is an integral part of the system. |
| Workflow | Compiere includes document level and process level workflow at its core. |
| eCommerce / WebStore integration | An integrated Java JSP webstore is included in the core release. |
| Data and SOA Integration | Transacting with different systems than your own through Electronic Data Interchange (EDI) or Web Services. Compiere offers this as part of its Enterprise Edition release, and his functionality can also be purchased through the Compiere Exchange. |

| Advanced Functionality | Description |
| --- | --- |
| **In-house Programming and Customization** | Usually, an end-user has to pay for the privilege of doing in-house programming on their purchased ERP systems. Being open source, this is given with Compiere. |
| **Advanced Material Resources Planning (MRP / MRP II)** | This is an additional paid-for Compiere component and offers an integrated MRP process. Functionalities including, route planning, resource scheduling, standard operations, and multi level Bills of Materials. |
| **Advanced Warehousing and Distribution** | This is an additional paid-for Compiere component and encompasses advanced warehousing and distribution systems. |
| **Human Resources** | This is an additional paid-for Partner component. |
| **Government ERP** | Fund Management is an additional paid-for Partner component. |

 Where applicable, the partner components contact details can be obtained from Compiere directly, or from the Compiere Exchange at the following web address: http://www.compiere.com/partners/compiere-exchange.

# Critical ERP decision factors

One of the most critical components in an Enterprise decision process is to ensure that all factors are considered in the evaluation process.

Such factors must include the following:

# Budget

Does the enterprise have an allocated budget for the ERP system? Does this budget include licensing, implementation, training, first year support, and, most importantly, up-front pre-evaluation functionality and scope design. Does the enterprise understand what is available in the market prior to setting this budget, and including management scope risks in this process?

What does the ERP budget mean to the organization? Is it a target cost or a strategic fund allocation?

Is the budget agreed with your implementation partner? Usually, if the scope is well-defined with good functional definition, then consulting partners will be happy, and budget should not be a concern. If management is under pressure from a budget point of view, quality may be compromised, and inevitably corners will be cut during the implementation.

Make sure you spend money to save money!

# Up-front functional design and data relationships

Don't purchase an ERP system if you have not created a Functional Design of how you want your business to work, or have at least documented how it currently works. Scope creep is usually a major risk factor in any implementation. The reason for this is poor up-front investigation and understanding by management—not of the ERP system, but of the business processes itself.

An Enterprise is measured according to data information and relationships. Document your data relationship entities in as much detail as possible. This does not require a database analyst but will at least ensure that most critical data relationships are identified up-front. Later in the book we will describe the entity relationships in Compiere.

# Static out-of-the-box versus dynamic flexible ERP

ERP systems that are more out-of-the-box are usually less flexible. More flexible systems are less out-of-the box.

How important is flexibility now, and what is the experience of the company in its historical systems? Owner-managed businesses require much more immediate flexibility in their systems purely because there is less bureaucracy in the decision-making process and their ground level understanding are much higher. "Safe" decision makers will require a more out-of-the-box solution since this offers a perceived level of comfort.

# Internal learning curve and time availability

Managing the internal learning curve is one of the most important aspects of the implementation. The more experienced management is in ERP systems, the easier it will be to manage the learning curve. What is usually quite interesting is that inexperienced management in this area will pay for the system but only want to see the results of the system and not understand what is under the hood.

"Hands-off management" should be aware that the implementation runs a huge risk of failure. It is quite surprising that management will outsource the entire process of implementation and only try to get involved in the end of the project, when the hand-over needs to happen. This is usually too late, and by then the expectation level runs the risk of being out of sync between the ERP implementer and the client.

If senior management don't have the time or inclination to be involved then no matter what system it is, it is going to have its internal political and project challenges throughout the process.

# Enterprise readiness

Although ERP changes affect the entire organization, in most circumstances, change is effected through the organization through simple, fast, clear, constant, and concise management decisions and communications.

Employees look up to their management, and key management or owners who have buy-in to the process are worth 100 times more than employee hand-holding sessions.

If the key management is change averse, then simply don't implement an ERP System.

# Technology

One of the drivers of the new age is technology. Investing in an ERP system is usually a significant investment. If you are going to invest in a technology , then you should make sure that you understand the underlying technologies of the systems that are going to run those systems.

Technology and proprietary platforms can become out of date or be difficult or even impossible to upgrade or integrate into other systems. Ultimately, the average career for employees is shorter than the technology that is going to be around. In your next organization, you are going to be stuck with the decisions of prior management, and the same truth will prevail about your legacy.

# Personal career aspirations

Personal aspirations and career ambitions form quite an interesting dynamic in the entire decision process, and must not be discounted. Employees can be very biased towards their own personal ambitions in terms of technology. Independent thinking should prevail wherever possible.

# Brand Loyalty

Take note that most existing brands have been in existence for almost 40 years and in most cases are the sum of diverse acquisitions, and the agility of these brands to adapt to changes in the technology space is recognized to be a major challenge. Evaluate brand loyalty for its emotional or real value context.

 Prioritize the selection factors and make sure that you get buy-in from all stakeholders.

# Do you evaluate Compiere differently because it is open source?

In evaluating Compiere the question is—should it be evaluated differently because it is open source? In short the answer is: No! However, in understanding the environment, there are many deciding factors and risks to consider when evaluating open source systems in general. Here are some areas to assess:

# It must meet your functional needs

Functionally, the ERP software must meet your needs, and must at least have passed your evaluation criteria through either proof of concept or proven functionalities.

# It must offer the Assurance Support Levels to suit your needs

Compiere offers traditional open source **General Public License (GPL)** software as well as commercially licensed and supported versions of the application. The user thus has a choice.

## Community-supported edition

Compiere offers a GPL version of their software as a community edition. In its simplistic form it is a form of distribution and exposure of the product to the world at large. In its complex form it is a collaborative, distributed, and transparent development environment. Community editions are good for evaluation, and small-to-medium environments until larger product support and upgrade assurances are required. Because the core of the product editions are the same, this book will cover both the community and paid-for editions.

## Paid-for enterprise editions

The enterprise versions of Compiere are certified to be standards-compliant from a software, database, and operating system point of view. Managed by seasoned executives, Compiere invested more into these Enterprise editions for commercial operational acceptance and they are the true, supported versions of the software:

- You can purchase support assurance for such versions, including certified upgrades and maintenance, from the software vendor
- You can rely on the stability and roadmap of the technology stack
- You can manage the responsiveness of the vendor contractually
- You can find certified local support and experience
- You can find training and documentation
- You can still benefit both from the community editions and input
- You can have indemnity against possible patent infringements

# It must provide an open source advantage

As the open source market is maturing, and while the open source evangelists and the proprietary shareholders each have their stake in the ground, when it comes to sound commercial and risk management decisions the technology environment is now about long term freedom of use, architecture and platform, and not about "free" software.

Within the Compiere environment, the underlying core source code and Java technology is open to inspect and expand upon. Compared to other environments, it is also easy to find developers and support within the Java and Oracle/Postgress database environment. It is impossible to cover the Java J2EE framework environment in conjunction with this book, but is regarded as one of the most prolific and matured development environments available today, and forms the core to technology companies like IBM and Oracle.

The business benefit is that the underlying business logic source code is transparent and it is possible to understand and match it to the precise business functional process.

No integration process is easy, but open source systems provide a dynamic integration with other systems purely from the fact that it is transparent from the technology stack point of view.

# Compiere editions

The different licensing options available to end users are as follows:

| Edition | Overview |
|---------|----------|
| Compiere Community | • Core ERP functionality<br>• Model-driven Application Platform<br>• Platform-independent client-server architecture<br>• GPL v2 open source license |
| Compiere Standard | • Stable and supported versions with quality support, bug fixes, and service packs<br>• Automated migration to latest versions<br>• Traditional Client/Server presentation<br>• Commercial license |
| Compiere Professional | • Advanced rich internet web UI architecture<br>• Additional enterprise-level functionality<br>• Premium support services<br>• EULA with indemnification protection<br>• Commercial license |
| Compiere Enterprise | • Multi server support<br>• Visual Editor and Management Dashboards<br>• RESTful Webservices<br>• Commercial license |

**Additional Paid-for Features:** Compiere Cloud Editions, Compiere Manufacturing, Compiere Warehouse, and Distribution.

In all editions, source code is supplied under different license agreements.

# Getting more information

Compiere has an extensive partner eco-system across the world, with up to 40 countries listed, across all continents. Partners provide a localized contact and support system for the Compiere system. The main aim of the partner community is to provide the following services:

- Sales
- Solution design
- Customization
- Implementation
- Ongoing support, maintenance, and upgrades
- System integration
- Industry specialization

A comprehensive list of partners available per country is available in the online partner directory, at: `http://www.compiere.com/partners/partner-directory`.

# Getting Compiere

To review purchasing options and download Compiere, you can go to `http://www.compiere.com/products/compare-editions/` for a comprehensive overview. To download Compiere Community, refer to `http://sourceforge.net/projects/compiere/files/`. For help on installing Compiere, and documentation on Compiere, please refer to: `http://wiki.compiere.com/`. For a trial version of the professional or enterprise editions please contact your local partner or Consona Corporation (www.consona.com) directly.

# Summary

Compiere emerged as a premier and leading open source ERP and a competitor to the traditional ERPs in the market due its technology stack and sound design principles. We covered the following in this chapter:

- The list of core functionalities in the Compiere system, as well as the advanced functionalities that are available.
- Evaluation criteria that you should use for the Compiere system. We highlighted the fact that you should prioritize these accordingly to your specific needs.
- Presented an understanding of the Compiere product offering options.
- Where to get more information, should you require in.

In the next chapter, we will illustrate the applicable setups required during initial implementation of a new tenant.

# 2
# The Initial Compiere Setup

Understanding the initial set-up process for an instance of Compiere is essential, because it forms the platform for the future use of the system.

In this chapter, we will illustrate the following:

- Introducing Compiere terminology and providing a set-up overview
- Creating an initial tenant
- Setting up the initial accounting elements (chart of accounts) and the accounting schema, which will form the basis for future document accounting
- Loading organizations and the applicable warehouses
- How to set up the document numbering sequences
- Highlight how to set up different unit of measure conversions
- How to create users and roles in the system

# Compiere Terminology

For purposes of the initial installation it is important to note the following terminology meanings:

| Terminology | Meaning |
| --- | --- |
| Tenant | A Tenant or client refers to the main instance name. You are not limited in the number of tenants, but you cannot share data between tenants. An example would be a GardenWorld Group instance. |
| Organization | Organization refers to the legal entities, Cost or Profit Centers, Departments, Divisions, or Top level Summary Organizations that may be applicable. You can share data between organizations. An example would be a head office and multiple stores. |
| Business Partners | This refers to customers, vendors, or employees with which the organization transacts. |
| Products | Products are stocked or non-stocked inventory items, expense items, or service items that you purchase and sell or track. |
| Accounting Schema | These are the default accounts that define the default accounting posting rules per Tenant or Organization. These include, for example, currency and costing rules. |
| Account Element | This defines the natural account key, number/Reference, and name that you will use as your accounting posting entry and that makes up the Chart of Accounts. This is, for example, account 6500-Telephone Expense. |
| Role | A role defines the window, process, and data access of users in the system. This could, for example, be a Sales Department Role. |
| Users | Users either have roles — in which case they are system users — or if they do not have a role they are referred to as contacts. |
| Representatives | Representatives are used on Compiere sales and purchasing documents, and the term refers to users that are defined as employees in the system. |
| Warehouse or Service Point | Warehouses are used for materials management, and an organization must have a warehouse assigned to it if inventory tracking is applicable. |

# Compiere setup overview

The instructions for the file installation process are detailed in the installation guides that can be obtained from `http://www.compiere.com/support/installation.php`.

After installing the database, Java run time, and Compiere, the Compiere environment setup can be started by running the program `RUN_setup`. This can be found under your main installation directory, as `c:\Compiere2\RUN_setup.bat` (Windows) or `/home/Compiere2/RUN_setup.sh` (Linux):

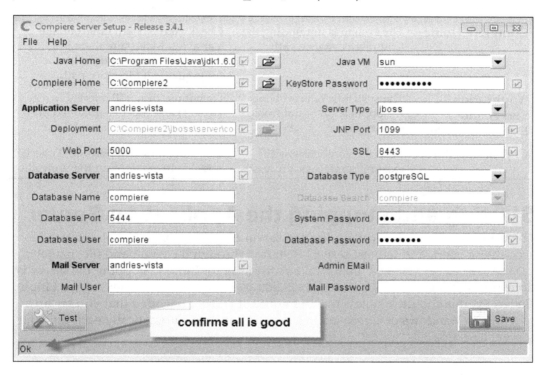

Should you experience problems with the above, the following common faults and solutions may be identified:

| Fault | Description | Resolution |
|---|---|---|
| **Java Home** | The system cannot find the fully qualified Java JDK path. | Check your Java installation and ensure that it is listed in your System Environment Variables. Make sure there is a JAVA_HOME entry pointing to the correct path. |
| **Compiere Home** | The system is not finding the Compiere instance path. | Check your System Environment Variables. Make sure there is a COMPIERE_HOME entry with the fully-qualified directory path. |
| **Application Server and Database Server** | The system is not resolving the application or database server. | Do not use direct IP references (i.e. 10.0.0.1) and must be qualified in your DNS or system's host file. |
| **Conflicting Ports** | Ports are conflicting with existing services or processes | Try using different ports, and check possible restrictions on the firewall. |

# Starting and stopping the Application Server

The Compiere JBoss, Tomcat application server (required for your web interface, accounting, alert, and request server) is started through the command file, namely C:\Compiere2\utils\RUN_Server2.bat file (.sh for Linux). Stopping the server is done through the c:\Compiere2\utils\RUN_Server2Stop.bat file (.sh for Linux). Generally, this should take less than a minute. It is recommended that you set up a schedule in Windows or a cron job in Linux to start this automatically each time the server starts up.

# Launching Compiere and logging in

There are two ways to log into the system:

## Desktop launch

On the server or workstation itself, as either the System Administrator or a user, this is traditionally done through a launch file in your Compiere directory — namely C:\Compiere2\RUN_Compiere2.bat (Windows) or .sh (Linux). After the initial log in, the user has a choice to create an icon shortcut on the desktop linking to this file for future use. In this method Compiere itself needs to be installed on the Desktop.

# Web launch

The recommended method for remote client/server login, where Compiere installation files need not be installed on the desktop is to run Compiere through the Java Webstart from an Internet browser launch page after you have started the Compiere Application Server. The access web page is accessed through `http:// < server name > : < web port > /admin`, where `<server name>` is your actual server name and `<web port>` is the web port defined in the `RUN_Setup` process followed by the `/admin` directory. An example of this would be `http://compiere-server.gardenworld.com:5000/admin`. Compiere will download the run-time files to the user desktop for use, and will always be of the latest instance avoiding possible version or maintenance conflict.

Click on the **Webstart** button to launch the Swing User Interface (UI) application (Community and Standard Editions), or access the Web User Interface (UI) through the **Compiere Web Application Login** selection (Professional and Enterprise Editions):

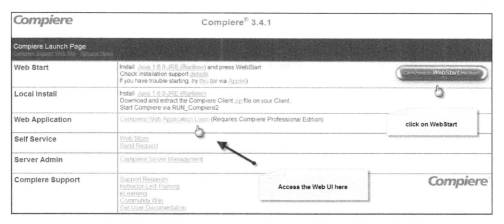

Enter your System Administrator username and password (refer to the installation documentation for the defaults) for the Swing version, as shown below:

Enter your System Administrator username and password (refer installation documentation for the default), for the Web UI version:

# The Compiere menu and windows

The Compiere menu launches the transactional aspects of the system and we will describe the different components as follows:

# The Compiere menu

Depending on your login credentials and role access, you will be presented with the main menu in Compiere. This menu lists your roles and actions that you may perform.

The Swing Menu (Community and Standard Editions) is illustrated as follows:

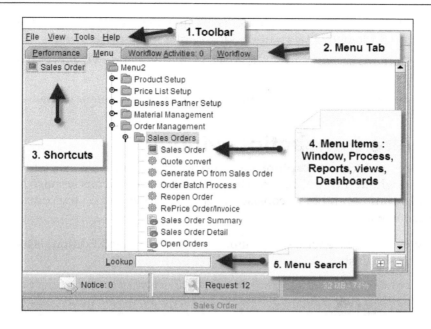

The Web User Interface (Professional and Enterprise Editions) is as follows:

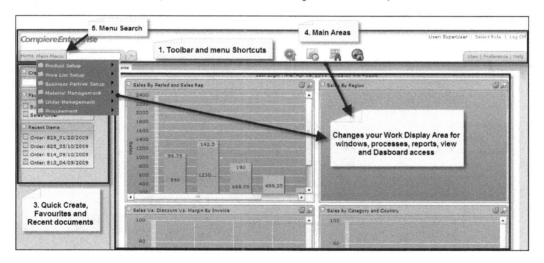

1.  **Toolbar and Menu Shortcuts**: These provide available predefined shortcuts, commands, and preferences.

2.  **Menu Tab**: These are available context menus or functions, such as performance dashboards, menu, workflow activities

3. **Shortcuts and Favorites**: Shortcuts are quick launch options, and are added to the shortcut area by right-clicking on the select menu item.

4. Menu items access your work areas, including windows, process, reports, views, and Dashboards.

5. **Menu Search**: This is where the user can search for menu items.

# Compiere transaction window

Windows are used for data capture and processing, and have a consistent look and feel throughout the application. The menu toolbar and icons are also located in standard positions and have consistent functionality based on the context of the contents of the window.

The Swing user interface window (Community and Standard Edition) is as shown in the following screenshot:

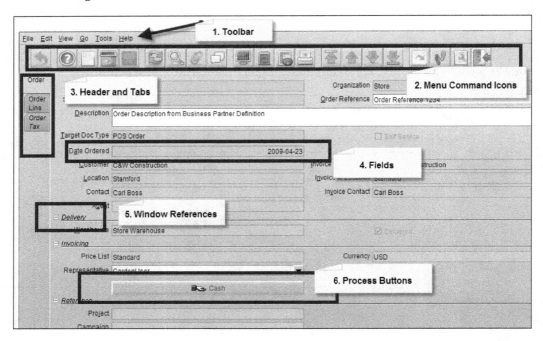

The web user interface window (Professional and Enterprise Edition) is as shown in the following screenshot:

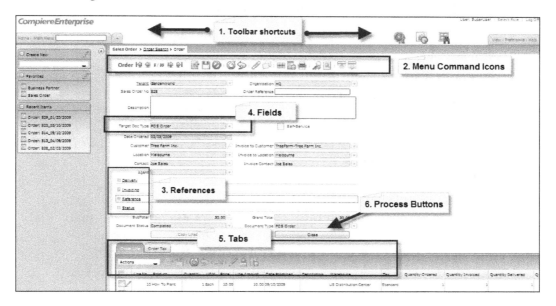

- **Toolbar**: The toolbar list shortcuts to commands and other windows, preferences, and set-up actions.

- **Menu icons**: The menu icons in Compiere launch commands in context to the contents of the window, for instance create new record, delete record, refresh, lookup, next record, previous record, and close window.

- **Header and Tabs**: A header is the first main view in a window, whereas tabs are contextualized to the header or preceding tab. For instance, an Order Header will have an Order Lines tab, and Order Lines will have Order Tax lines.

- **Fields**: Fields capture the contents of a document, may be mandatory and may be editable, depending on context.

- **Window References**: Creates a context of fields on a window. If pressed, shortens the window.

- **Process buttons**: These buttons perform actions and processes depending on the context. For instance, on and order you may process a payment type against it or complete a document.

# Initial set-up process

The following basic steps apply to setting up a Compiere instance:

- Define the initial Chart of Accounts (account elements) template for the tenant.
    - ○ Create the tenant instance to hold your Compiere data.
    - ○ Define your calendar year and periods.
    - ○ Populate and define the data structures of the following:
        - ○ Organizations, Warehouses, Bank, Cash Books, and Unit of measures.
        - ○ Accounting schema, account elements, currencies, and charges.
        - ○ Accounting set-ups of Business Partner Groups, Product Categories, Tax, Projects, Works Orders, bank accounts, cash books, and warehouses.
        - ○ Document types, Document Sequences, Payment Terms, and Sales Regions
        - ○ Define system users and access roles.

# Defining the account elements (Chart of Accounts) import

Prior to setting up a new tenant, the account elements (Chart of Accounts) must be defined as per the import template provided. The standard account elements template can be found in the `C:\Compiere2\data\import` directory. The template used as the default during the installation process is named `AccountingUS.xls`, and the default import file template is named `AccountingUS.csv` (note that there may be other localized templates defined for other countries). The process is that you could edit either the `.xls` file or the `.csv` file, but it is the `.csv` format layout that is used for the import process.

The following columns are defined in the Account Element Template, and although they are defined vertically here. these must be defined horizontally in your import file. This may be imported before or after an initial tenant is created. Do plan these fields carefully, as this is a structure used for Financial Reporting and your accounting reports.

| Column No | Name | Description |
|---|---|---|
| 1 | Account Value | Account Values are the numeric numbering of your accounts. You should adopt some sequential logic as this will benefit you greatly in reporting and structure down the line: I propose the following numbering sequence, based on IFRS reporting: |
| | | 000..999 Use these for your Summary levels |
| | | 10000...19999 Assets |
| | | 20000...29999 Liabilities |
| | | 30000...39999 Owners Equity and Reserves |
| | | 40000...49999 Revenue |
| | | 50000...59999 Cost Of Sales |
| | | 60000...69999 Staff related Expenses |
| | | 70000....79999 Operating Expenses |
| | | 80000....89999 Taxation and Shareholders Expense |
| | | 90000....99999 Miscellaneous |
| | | An example of this would be: |
| | | 4-Trade Revenue |
| | | 480-Revenue Other  [ being a summary level ] |
| | | 48000-Revenue Other account 1 |
| | | 48010-Revenue Other account 2 |
| 2 | Account Name | This is the name of the account or Summary Level Account |
| 3 | Account Description | A further description of the account |
| 4 | Account Type | Compiere defines five standard account types: |
| | | Assets, Liabilities, Owner's Equity, Revenue, Expenses |
| 5 | Account Sign | The account sign, namely Positive, Negative, or Neutral. Use Neutral if you are unsure. |

| Column No | Name | Description |
| --- | --- | --- |
| 6 | Account Document | Yes/No indicating if the account is document controlled, in which case journal entries may not be posted to this account. Certain system control accounts , such as bank-in-transfer and Accounts Receivable/Payable, should be indicated as document controlled. |
| 7 | Account Summary | Yes/No indicating whether the account is a summary level account or not. Summary level accounts are used for roll-up reporting. |
| 8 | Default Account | Indicates that this is a default account used for the accounting schema rules. Generally, these can be understood from their name and there is a predefined list of accounts within the import template. Compiere will release a new template if these accounts changes. |
| 9 | Account Parent | This indicates the account parent number of the account line.<br><br>For instance, if 4 is defined as the Revenue summary account then an account 4000 Revenue Trade would be parented by 4, which in itself may be a parent of another account. |

# Setting up a tenant

To setup the initial tenant you have to log into the system with the **SuperUser** username, and select the role of **System Administrator**:

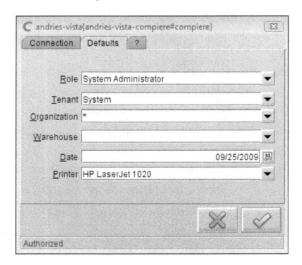

Select the **Initial Tenant Setup** from the menu, and enter your tenant details as follows:

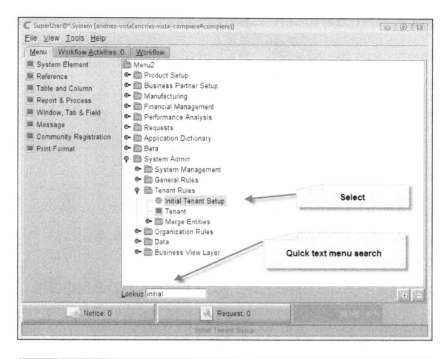

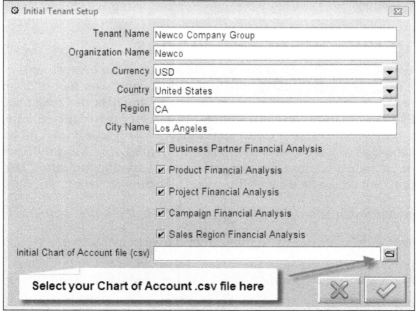

Now that you have set up a tenant, the following system items are created through this process (these can be easily edited):

- **Initial organizational admin and user roles**: In the above example, this is Newco Company Group Admin and Newco Company Group User. The admin role so created will be the administrator for the tenant.

- Accounting Schema and Account Elements.

- An Initial Campaign, Business Partner, Business Partner Group, Product, Product Category, Tax, Representative (Admin and User), Project, and Cash book.

- Document types applicable to the system, together with standard numbering sequences.

 After you have run the initial Tenant Setup in the System Administration role, log out and log back into the system using the particular new tenant credentials.

# Defining the calendar, year, and periods

A calendar and periods define the reporting and posting dimension of the system entries. An initial calendar, a year, and periods are created, and may be edited. This information is set up through the **Calendar, Year,** and **Period** menu item, and is covered in Chapter 6.

# Setting up your organizations

Organizations can be defined according to your business and reporting line requirements. Organizations can be used for security purposes as well, for instance having a separate 'accounts' organization for accounting data that may not be accessed by sales organization staff , but never used for organizational reporting. One of the powerful features of Compiere is that these organizations and hierarchy may be changed at any time, with future reporting trees or roll-ups reflected in the new set-up. In more advanced reporting scenarios, a specific **Reporting Hierarchy** may be set up which can be use for **Financial Reporting** (covered in Chapter 6).

Setting up your organization:

1. Select the **Organization** window from the main menu tree.

2. Enter your Organization's Search key, Name, and Description. These can be the same if there is no reason to distinguish between them for future reporting.

3. Enter your Organization, and flag it at Summary level if that is applicable.

4. Move the Organizations around with your mouse to indicate the correct parent-child relationship in the tree. You can have multiple reporting summary levels under each other, and are not limited in the depth of this tree.

5. Validate the Organization, in order to create the appropriate costing records for the organization.

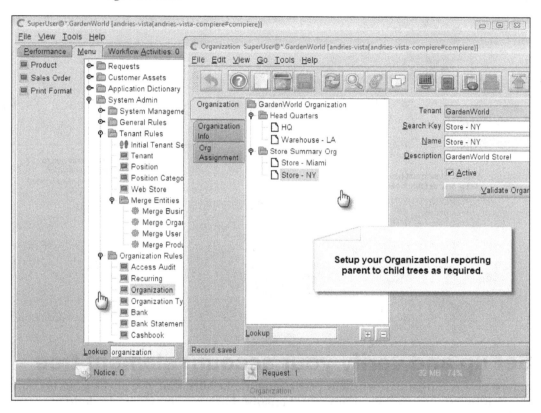

# Setting up your warehouses and locators

Warehouses are used for the inventory management of stock items. Warehouses are a central control point for:

- Material Receipt from a Vendor, and Customer Shipment transactions
- Cost accounting for products is at warehouse level
- Replenishment of products in the system is at warehouse level

You may have multiple warehouses per organization, and for each warehouse you may have multiple locators:

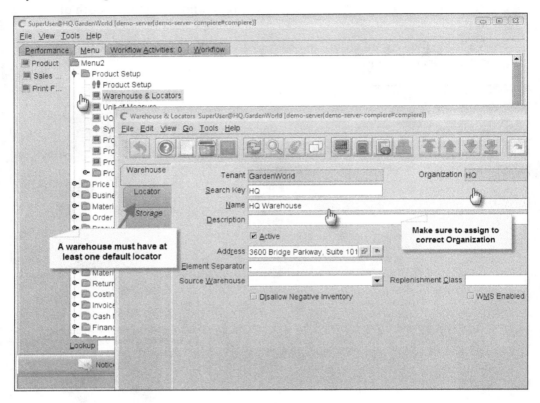

# Set up and verify your account element tree

Before performing any document processing, make sure that you check your account element tree (hierarchy) structures, and ensure that these are properly defined. Although Compiere allows the element tree to be changed, it saves a lot of time down the line if it is correct from the start, so it is advised to do this up-front.

This is done through the **Account Element > Element Value** window/tab:

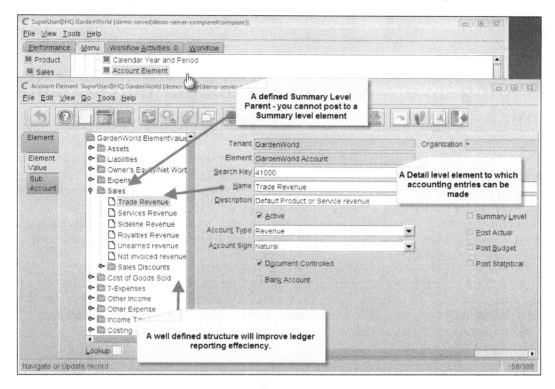

The Account Elements tree is defined through the imported account parent, and within Compiere is manually changed or moved appropriately to its parent. Some important notes on the set-up of account elements are:

- **Document Controlled:** This means that General Journal entries (non document transactions) will not be able to be posted to this account.

- **Bank Account:** This flag indicates whether this account relates to a Bank account. A bank account must be selected for such accounts.

- **Summary level:** If the account element is a summary level account used for reporting purposes, then you cannot post to it.

- **Post Actual / Budget / Statistical:** These types of posting can be made to this account through Journal entries.

As part of the initial set-up process you must set up a Bank account through the Bank window in Compiere. This is done through the **Bank** Window.

# Setting up and verify your accounting schema rules

The accounting schema defines the rules set-up for default accounting principles. Most importantly, an accounting schema must be set up for each reporting currency, which is referred as the Accounted Currency. Should more than one reporting currency be applicable – for instance in multiple countries – then multiple accounting schemas must be set up. GAAP Accounting principles indicate that only one reporting currency is generally required per country, so then only one accounting schema is required. Managing multiple accounting schemas is a tricky process and not advisable unless you have such legal requirements.

Where there are multiple currencies, the accounting currency will be the currency defined in your Accounting Schema for transacting purposes (see below). Source currencies may vary, and all source currencies are converted through currency rates to the Accounted Currency. Currency rates are set up through the **Currency Rate** window.

## Accounting Schema overview

The Accounting Schema defines the following:

- **Accounting GAAP:** Which Accounting GAAP in in place and the specific rules applicable to it. Contact your implementation partner for such custom requirements.

- **Commitment type:** With regards to commitment accounting – this would indicate the accounting for sales and purchase order commitments as accrued Revenue or Expenses. An implementation of this will require further customization from standard.

- **Costing method:** Various costing methods are available, including Standard Costing, Average PO, Average Invoice, Last Invoice, FIFO, LIFO, and Last PO price. Standard Costing and Average Invoice are the most commonly-used. Other options will require detailed customization.

- **Costing level:** Indicates at what level the costing method will be used, including Organization (thus Warehouse), Batch or Lot, or Tenant level (highest level).

- **Currency:** The accounting currency for this accounting schema.

- **Automatic period control:** This automatically opens a Period Control window period in the system for document processing, say 30 days prior and 30 days after the current system date.

- **Tax correction:** This defines the tax accounting correction level for write-off and discount entries during payment allocation.

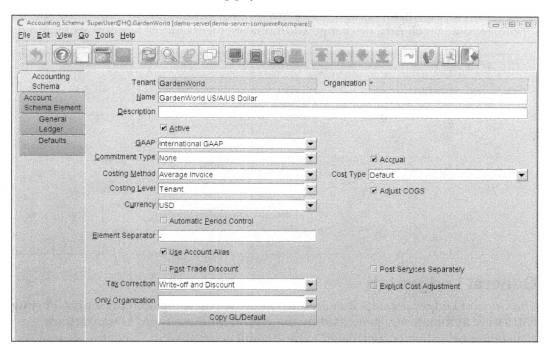

## Account schema elements (Information Dimensions) tab

Accounting schema elements are derived from the transactional document. Where a particular transactional document has accounting consequences, the data needs to be populated based on the following available information dimensions:

- Organization
- Natural Account
- Product
- Business Partner
- Marketing Campaign
- Sales Region
- Project

- Activity
- Location From / To
- Budget
- Sub Account
- User custom fields (2)

In its most basic form, an account element's debits and credits must balance at the Organizational level. Add or change additional elements in this window as required:

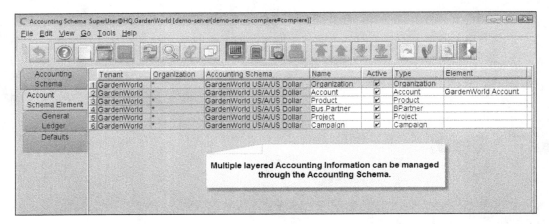

## General Ledger tab

The General Ledger defaults lists the suspense and balancing account setups. Posting entries are automatically generated by the system for these types of transactions, i.e. a suspense balancing entry created to the default account where a contra account is not listed by the user.

## Defaults tab

These accounts are the tenant's default account elements used by the document transactions during processing, and when creating, for instance, business partners, products, warehouses, projects, and banks. As mentioned before, these accounts are populated during the import of the initial account elements template.

Changes that are made to the default accounts can be copied by the user through their affected related default accounts, as follows:

- Business Partner Groups are updated with the new default accounts
- Product Categories are updated with the new default accounts
- Bank account defaults are updated or overridden
- Cash journal defaults are updated or overridden
- In addition to the above, the default accounts for tax, projects, and works orders (manufacturing) is updated or overridden.

## Account Combinations and aliases

Accounting Combinations are automatically generated account information about information dimension combinations, and by linking an alias to such combination, it can be used for faster entry during journal entries or accounting set-ups. In effect, you set up an alias that refers to a specific account combination for quick reference in the system.

Aliases for generated combinations can be manually created as follows, in the **Account Combination** window:

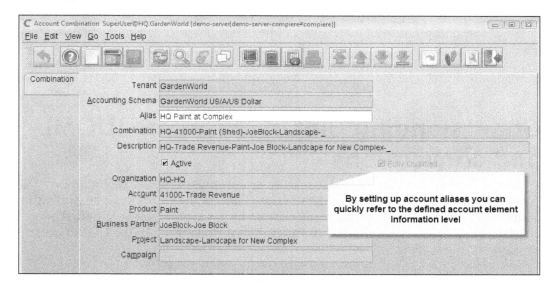

An example of using an alias for the above combination in an account setup of a charge is as follows:

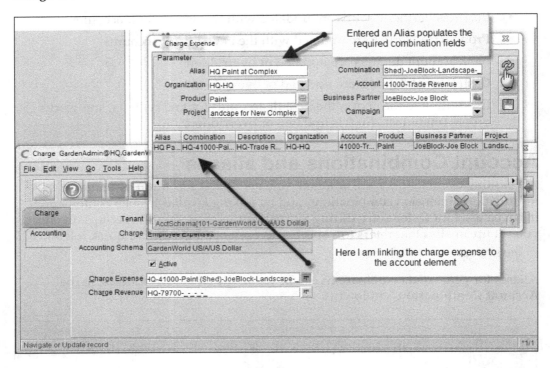

More detailed financial management aspects are covered in Chapter 6.

# Understanding Unit of Measures (UOM) and conversions

While the system is initially populated with various unit of measures that are pre-defined it is quite critical to understand that unit of measures must be explicitly defined for your instance. Unit of measures can be grouped together to define a set of related UOMs, i.e. Each-6Pack-Box-Pallet. This is done through the **UOM Group** menu item.

In the following example we are going to set up two additional unit of measures—namely litres and gallons, in order to illustrate the conversion between the two, for a sample product we shall call Diesel. In order to do this:

- Select the **Unit of Measure** window:
- Create a UOM with a **UOM code** and **Symbol** of 'L' and a Name of **Litre**.
- Create a UOM with a **UOM code** and **Symbol** of 'gal' and a Name of **Gallon**.
- Create a product in the **Product** window named **Diesel**, with a **unit of measure** of 'litre'.
- Return to edit the **UOM Liter**. On the **Conversion** tab, create a conversion from **Litre** to **Gallon** with a **multiply rate** of **0.264172** for product **Diesel**. The system automatically calculates the divide rate correctly.

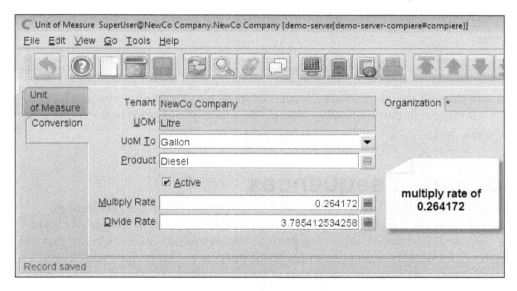

Multiply rates and divide rates indicate the calculation to be used for the conversion between units of measure. It is important that they be explicitly defined. For example, if conversions from litres to gallons and litres to kilolitres exists, gallons to kilolitres will not be calculated by the system and must be defined in its own right.

During processing of this product in Sales, Purchasing, and Materials transactions you will then be able to select either of the unit of measures set up, and any quantity entered will be converted accordingly.

For example, **Litre** selected for transaction (assuming a list price of 100 for a liter of diesel):

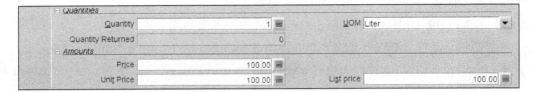

If the UOM is then changed to **Gallon** on the transaction, then the following values are used:

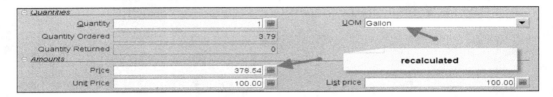

You will thus be able to transact in either of these two UOMs for this product, and Compiere will automatically convert the quantity and price to the applicable UOM selected.

# Document sequences

Particular Document Types in Compiere have specific Document Sequences, which are created during initial tenant setup. You may wish to change or create new (advised) document sequences prior to any system documents being processed, in order to control these sequences for audit purposes. This is done as follows:

1. Select the **Document Sequence** window.

2. Find and select the applicable **Document Sequence** that you wish to change. For example, let's select the **AR Invoice** document type.

3. Select and change the document sequence by editing the **Prefix** field, and add the words **INV** to the document sequence number.

4. From version 3.6 of Compiere, a handy **Gapless** flag is provided which, if selected, allows for internal IDs to be in numerical sequence in all instances. If this field is not selected, then IDs may have sequence gaps.

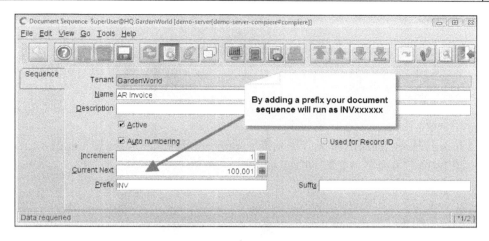

# Creating a user

During the initial phases of a Compiere installation, you will need to create user access roles and the user detail. Users may not necessarily have a User Role assigned to them. Such users are referred to as Contacts. If this field users have roles assigned to them they will be able to log in to the system and perform tasks that are allowed, as per their Role access level.

Users are created through the **User** menu item, which opens to the following window:

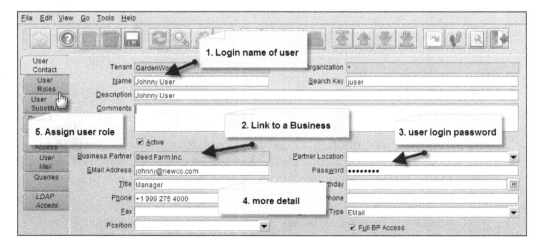

The basic steps in creating a user are as follows:

1. Assign the user a login name. This must be unique.

2. Link to a Business Partner. Where users are employees of the company, it is suggested that you create a Business Partner with the same name, but defined as an Employee.

3. Assign the user a password.

4. Enter more informational details regarding the user, such as email address, phone, fax, and any other detail that may be required.

5. Assign a role to the user:

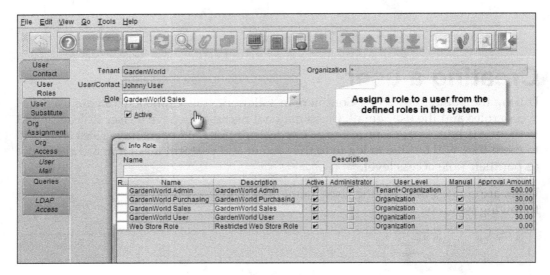

# Set up roles

Setting up roles requires some planning in the system, as you would want to avoid too many inconsistent roles to manage. It is recommended that these closely match the organization's job description to a functional level. In normal circumstances, similar users with similar job functions will have access to the same roles in the system. Within role access management, you can define the following (see **Role** window below):

- **Org Access tab**: Roles may be used to manage the role's organizational access (**Role** window), or a user can be individually assigned in terms of their organizational access (**User** Window).

- **User Assignment tab**: You may define which Users have access to the Role.

- **Window access**: You may define, per window, what read and write access this role defines.

- **Process access**: Processes are items like reports or specific processes such as creating orders or invoices. This is done at the transactional level.

- **Form access**: There exist certain custom windows that are referred to as Forms in the system, because they are more complex. An example of this may be the payment allocation or the workflow activity form.

- **Workflow access**: You may define which users have access to which workflows.

- **Task access**: You may define which users have access to pre-defined tasks.

- **Business View Layer (BVL) access**: You may define the specific Business Views that users may have access to (Compiere Professional version 3 and above).

- **Dashboards and parameters access**: You may define the specific management dashboards that users may have access to (Compiere Enterprise version 3.5 and above).

# Creating a role

To create a role in the system you will have to perform the following:

1.  Log into the system using the Organization's Admin role, as this role has the access rights to manage roles. In our example, this would be **Newco Company AdminRole**:

2. Select the **Role** window

3. Create an example Role called **Purchase Order clerk**, as follows:

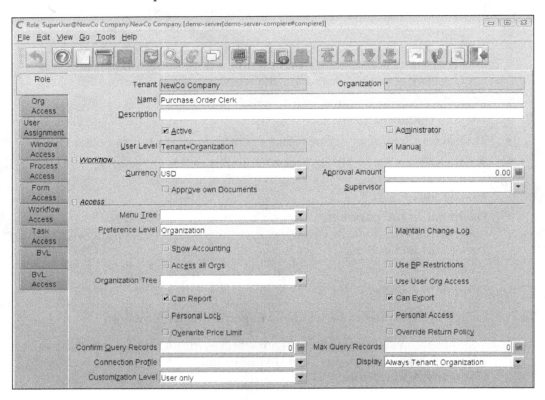

4. Within the **Role** window, you can select the appropriate access level to windows, processes, Forms, Workflow, Tasks, and Business views:

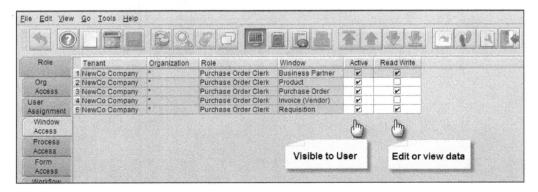

The access levels of shared Business Partners, Products, and Users are set up by using the (*) Organization, and with the appropriate role access defined as such. Warehouses must belong to an Organization, and may not be shared in this manner.

We will be covering more advanced aspects of roles in Chapter 7.

# Summary

Creating the Compiere Tenant is just the starting point, as this requires many other set-up steps that must be clarified before transaction processing can start. Such aspects include language packs, account charges, taxation, Business Partner Groups, and Product Categories.

During the initial installation process of Compiere you will have created a default database. This database contains the Compiere demo Tenant, data namely the *Garden World Demo Company*. We will be using this Tenant's data, and extending it for illustration purposes during subsequent chapters.

In this chapter you have learned:

- Compiere terminology and setup
- How to set up an initial tenant in the system, load the Organization Tree, and define Warehouses
- How to load and set up account elements and the accounting schema
- How to change unit of measures and document sequences
- How to set up a basic user and role

In the next chapter, we will illustrate Customer Relationship Management through the document transactions of the Sales Cycle.

# 3
# Customers and the Sales Process

Capturing your transactional relationships about and with Customers is a requirement for any successful sales organization. Managing your customer and sales process entails master data management, order fulfillment, invoicing, and linking to inventory shipment processes.

In this chapter we will illustrate the following:

- Defining Business Partners, credit management, and leads
- Overview of Sales Order to Invoice processing
- Dealing with different types of orders and their transactional implications
- How to generate Sales Invoices
- Open Orders, Invoice Inquiries, and Reporting on Sales
- Returns Management, and how commission calculations are facilitated
- Give an overview of the accounting consequences of Sales processing

The processes mentioned in this chapter are applicable to all versions of Compiere.

## The Sales Overview

In order to make sales you require information about the entity that you are doing business with, and you need to ensure that your processes reflect an efficient and effective way of transacting with your customer.

A scenario within Compiere would be where customers capture their details sales transaction through the Compiere web store. This would be illustrated as follows:

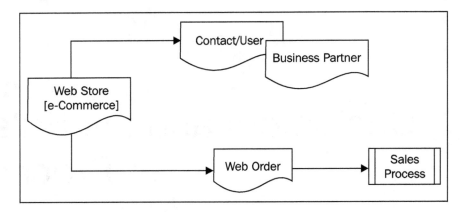

In the above scenario, the customer would capture their own details through the self service web store, and create their own orders.

The most typical scenario would be where the Compiere user captures details about Leads, Business Partners, and starts transacting, as illustrated:

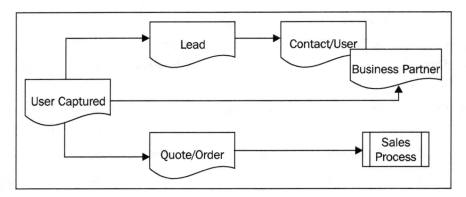

The Sales Cycle requires the following set-up flow:

- Business partners, Sales representatives, and optionally the Sales Region, Commission run, Marketing channel, and campaigns. Leads may also be captured and converted to Business Partners.
- Sales Order, Shipment, and Invoicing document types.
- In a new tenant setup with many new customers, Business Partners, and legacy Open Orders not yet fulfilled would be imported through import layouts. This process will not be covered in this book.

# Defining your business partners

Business partners are your Customers, Vendors, and Employees (or any combination of the three). Similar Business Partners are grouped into Business Partner Groups. Business partners may have one or more locations, contacts, and users attached to them. Business partners may also have special relationships in the form of proxy and linked business partners.

# Proxy business partners

This refers to proxy relationship scenarios where, for example, a store receives the goods and HQ gets invoiced and pays, or where the store receives the goods and is invoiced and HQ pays. This applies to both customers and vendors (material receipt) transactional scenarios.

# Linked organization business partners

This is a special type of business partner that is explicitly linked to organizations within Compiere in order to facilitate counter document processing. Counter document processing involves inter-organization transactions generated by the system automatically between linked business partners. For example, a store (linked to a Store Organization) raises a purchase order on the head office (also a linked HQ Organization) and the head office automatically generates a sales order counter document to the store.

Business partners are maintained through the business partner window in Compiere.

Setting up a business partner requires the following information to be entered:

1.  **The Business Partner Group**: This defines the Business Partner Group Names, accounting, and default parameters, including price lists, discount schemas, and return policies, as follows:

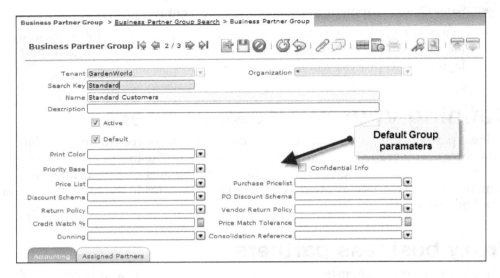

2.  **Payment terms**: Payment terms indicate the expected cash flow timing for a Business Partner document. The following screenshot shows the definition of a 2%10 Days net 30 payment term:

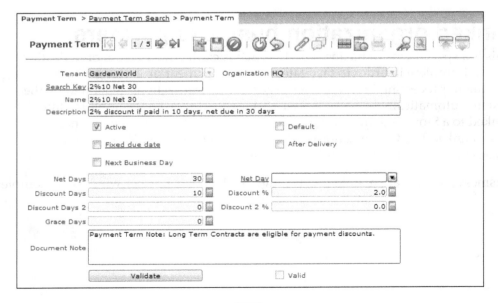

3. **Invoice schedule:** This determines the timing schedule for summary invoices. For instance, invoices are generated weekly for the delivery shipments for the week. This is not required if not used.

4. **Dunning** (Statement letters): Defines the set-up of dunning runs (Statement letters) to customers for collection purposes.

5. **Business Partner information:** Set up Business Partner information through the `Business Partner` window, which can be your customers, vendors, or employees (or a combination of the three). Link locations and contacts to your Business Partners here, as well:

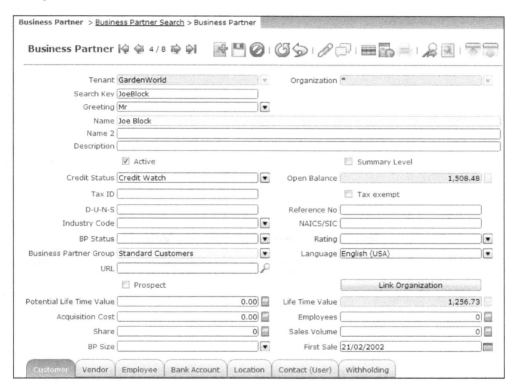

A Business Partner is identified as a customer through the **Customer** tab:

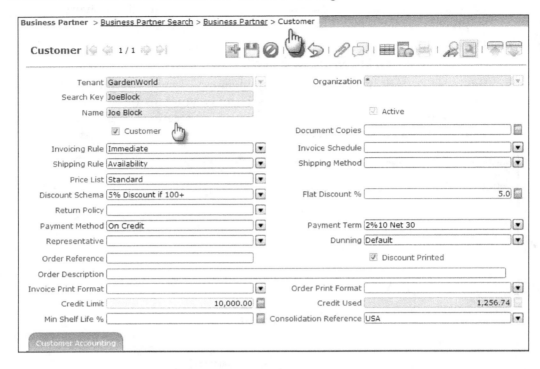

A Business Partner is identified as a vendor through the **Vendor** tab:

A Business Partner is identified as an employee through the **Employee** tab. Set up Sales Representatives by selecting indicating the **Sales Rep** field as follows:

A Business Partner may have multiple address locations as follows:

- **Pay-from:** Indicating the address from where a customer pays, and to which dunning statements should be sent.

- **Invoice address:** The address that is used for invoicing.

- **Ship to address:** The address for shipping documents.

- **Remit to address:** The payment remittance address.

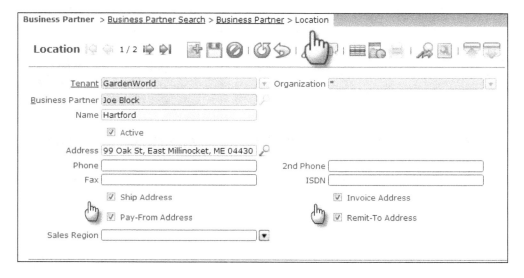

A Business Partner must always have at least one active location.

# Credit management

Credit management relates to managing your credit exposure with your customer through the sales cycle, including orders, invoicing, and shipment limit exposure. Credit limits are set up through the `Business Partner > Customer> Credit Limit` field:

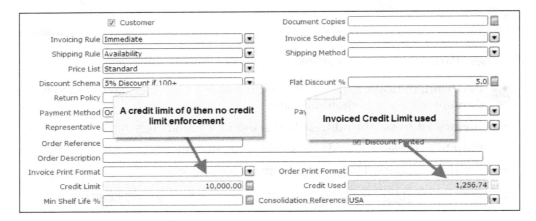

 Credit limits set to zero (0) value will indicate unlimited credit. The set in code style field indicates the balance of open invoices (balance of invoices not yet allocated to receipts).

Credit management is activated through the `Business Partner > Credit Status` field:

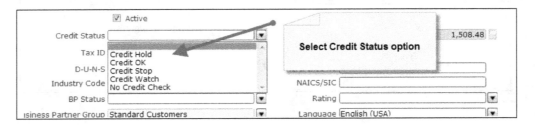

The **Credit Status** field parameters indicate the following:

- **Credit Hold**: Automatically set by the system when the credit balance is larger than the credit limit. No customer orders or shipments will be allowed.

- **Credit OK**: Credit Management is active and credit is OK.

- **Credit Stop**: This is a manual setting and no invoicing will be allowed.

- **Credit Watch**: Credit Management is active and the credit balance used is less than xx percent of credit limit allowable. The credit watch percent is set in the `Business Partner Group > Credit Watch` field.

- **No Credit Check**: No Credit Management is in place. All orders, shipments, and invoices are allowed.

# Entering leads and converting to business partners

The system allows for the entering of Sales Leads. Once a Sales Lead has been qualified, it can be converted into opportunities, contacts, and business partners (customers).

1. Enter Lead information through the `Lead` Window:

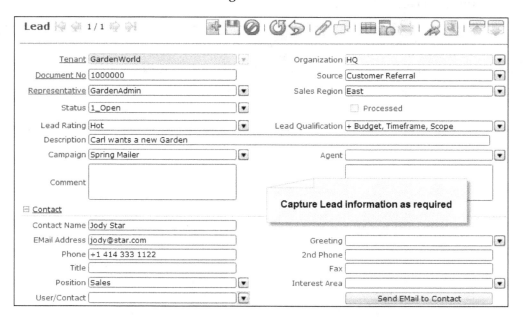

2. In the **Lead** window, create the Contact, Business Partner, Location, and convert to an Opportunity:

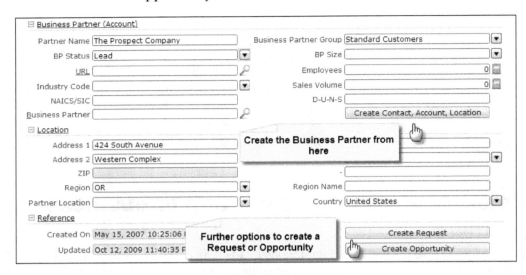

3. After the generation of this additional tracking information, the Compiere window tabs are displayed as follows, from which further data relevant to this lead can be tracked:

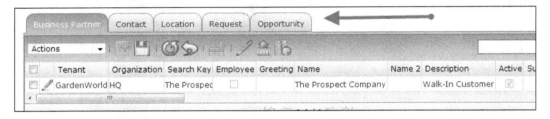

# Sales order to invoice processing

When following general best practices, Sales Order processing entails Quotations, Sales Orders, and Invoicing, which links to the inventory process of the shipment of goods to the customer. The menu options for sales processing are accessed through the Order Management menu item in Compiere:

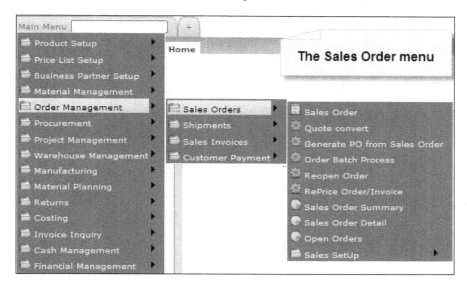

The Sales Order window is the originating Control Document in the sales process, from which other documents flow. An overview of the process is as follows:

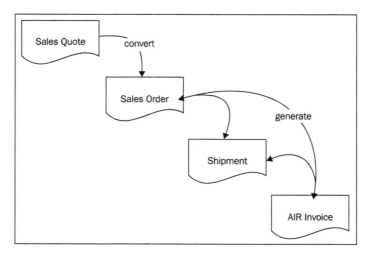

You can create a quote, copy or convert it to a Sales Order, and then generate the Shipment or Invoice individually or simultaneously. This all depends on the target document types selected during the processing. The standard document types that are created by the system are shown below:

| Document | Document Type | Narrative |
| --- | --- | --- |
| Proposal | Non-Binding Offer | Inventory is not reserved. |
| Quotation | Binding Offer | Inventory is reserved. |
| Sales Order | Standard Order | Batch-driven order. |
| | Warehouse Order | Shipment is auto-generated. |
| | On Credit Order | Shipment and Invoice are auto-generated. |
| | POS Order | Shipment and Invoice and Receipt are auto-generated. |
| | Prepayment | With a Prepayment, the shipment is only affected after Receipt is captured for the order. |
| | Web Order | An order captured from the self-service webstore. |
| Invoice Customer | AR Invoice | Sales Invoice is generated based on the Invoice rule. |
| | AR Credit Note | Sales Credit Notes are usually manually generated unless the Returns Management process is followed. |

Document types are defined through the Document Type window. Here are the settings for the **Standard Order** document type:

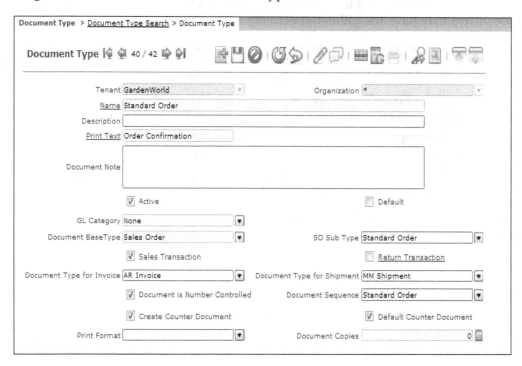

Capturing the target Sales Order document types from the Sales Order window:

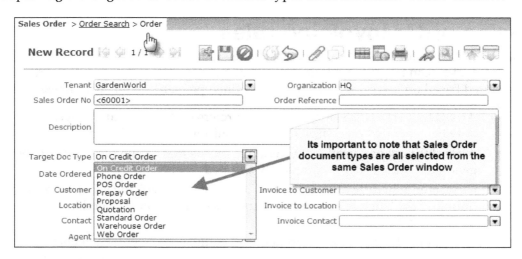

# Sales order delivery rules

Compiere allows for multiple shipments per order, depending on the delivery rules. Sales orders may have the following delivery rules selected:

- **Availability:** This is the default setting, and shipments are only generated when there is inventory available. Goods are automatically put on back-order if this option is selected, and this may lead to multiple shipments.

- **Complete Line/Order**: Only deliver based on the fulfillment of lines or a complete order.

- **After Receipt**: Only deliver after receipt of payment.

- **Force**: Force shipment even if it means negative stock on hand.

- **Manual**: Shipments will be manually captured. Products must, however, be set to exclude Auto Delivery.

Generating shipments can be by manual selection or through a batch process. Shipments are generated by the warehouse or by Business Partners, and can be consolidated.

Generating shipments to customers is described in more detail in Chapter 4.

# Sales order invoicing rules

Compiere allows for multiple invoices per order, and for certain order document types, invoices can be generated via a batch run or manually. These invoices are generated based on invoicing rules that are defined per sales order, as follows:

- **After Delivery**: This is the default, and refers to the fact that invoices will only be generated on completion of the shipment, per order line.

- **After delivery of complete Order:** This means that the invoice will only be generated if the order is completely shipped.

- **Customer Schedule after Delivery:** Based on the invoicing schedule and the timing of the batch run, shipments are rolled up to consolidated invoices up to that point in time.

- **Immediate**: Regardless of shipment status, the invoice will be generated. The only requirement in this scenario would be that the order has been completed.

# Manually generating invoices from orders

Manually generating invoices from Sales Orders is done through the `Generate Invoices (Manual)` window:

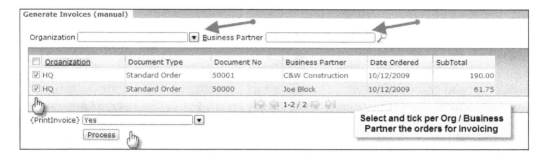

 Only orders of document type Standard or Warehouse can be generated in this manner.

# Batch generation of invoices

Invoices can be generated in batch through the `Generate Invoice` menu process:

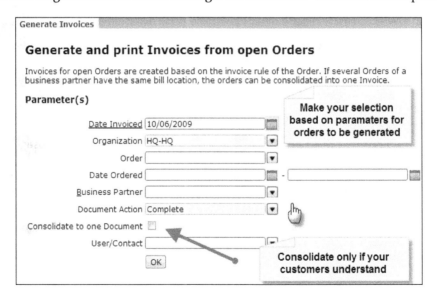

[  Only orders of document type Standard or Warehouse can be generated via the batch invoicing process. ]

# Document status and actions

Every document in Compiere has a Document Status. Document Actions refer to the document process to change the status of orders, shipments, and invoices (for instance to change the status from Draft to Completed). Except for system workflow status changes, document statuses are updated by the user. The general workflow status for an order is from Drafted to Prepare to Complete, and for an invoice would be from Drafted to Completed status. Once Completed, the document can be processed by the accounting engine, and the journal posting entry will be created.

| Status | Note | Sales Order | Shipment | Invoice |
|---|---|---|---|---|
| Draft | This is the most common state. Be careful of this document type as it is not a system processing state. | Edit state | Edit state | Edit state |
| Completed | Follow-on processing is allowed | Reserves Stock | Updates Stock values | Updates posting |
| Void | Not a recommended action as it reverses and nullifies the document | Nullify | Nullify | Nullify |
| Close | "Ends" the document for processing | Close | Close | Close |
| Reverse | Creates an opposite entry of the document | Reversal document generated | Reversal | Reversal |
| Re-activate | Only Completed documents can be re-activated | Editable | Editable | Editable |

A Drafted document status can be processed as follows:

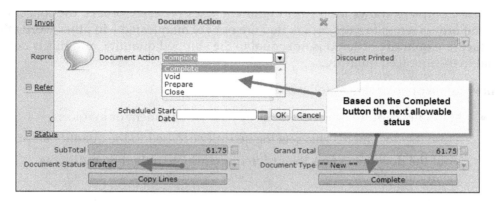

A Completed document status can be changed as follows:

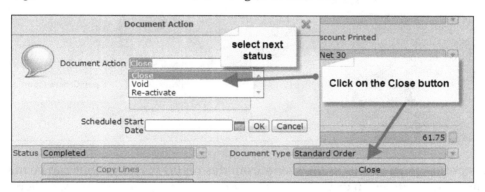

 The document type's calendar, year, and period must be open and active in order for the document action to be performed.

# Reporting on open orders

Because Compiere allows for the unfulfillment (back order) of orders, the concept of open orders refers to sales orders that are not yet manifested — in other words the product line quantity ordered is not equal to the shipped quantity, and this is not equal to the invoiced quantity.

Follow up on open orders as follows:

- Manually capture or generate the applicable shipment or invoice.
- Close the document: This sets the quantity ordered to the quantity shipped.
- Void the document: Sets the ordered quantity to 0 thereby nullifying the document.

The open order report is accessed through the **Open Orders** menu item:

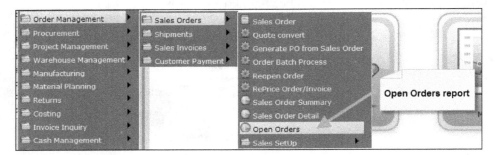

The report is generated as follows, and from this report investigations can be made to follow up on items, in order to invoice, or deliver or replenish from suppliers:

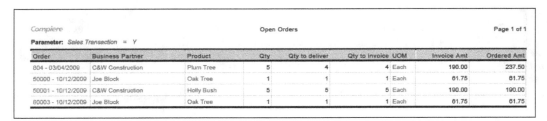

| Order | Business Partner | Product | Qty | Qty to deliver | Qty to Invoice | UOM | Invoice Amt | Ordered Amt |
|---|---|---|---|---|---|---|---|---|
| 804 - 03/04/2009 | C&W Construction | Plum Tree | 5 | 4 | 4 | Each | 190.00 | 237.50 |
| 50000 - 10/12/2009 | Joe Block | Oak Tree | 1 | 1 | 1 | Each | 61.75 | 61.75 |
| 50001 - 10/12/2009 | C&W Construction | Holly Bush | 5 | 5 | 5 | Each | 190.00 | 190.00 |
| 80003 - 10/12/2009 | Joe Block | Oak Tree | 1 | 1 | 1 | Each | 61.75 | 61.75 |

# Finding sales order documents

Finding current and historical documents in the system is easy. Compiere facilitates this through the following processes:

# Zoom on field names

This process involves right-clicking on a document link and then zooming into
the document.

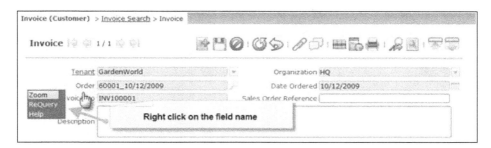

**Cross Document Zoom Reference**

Because the Sales Order is the control document in the Sales process, from the sales
order you can zoom across to your relevant document.

# Order info view

Compiere provides an info view on the transactional documents of the system. These
can be accessed from anywhere in the system and then viewed or zoomed into from
the info view windows.

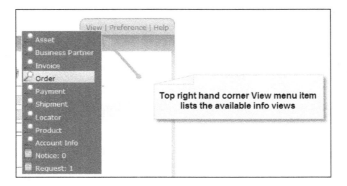

The displayed info view menu item is as shown in the following screenshot:

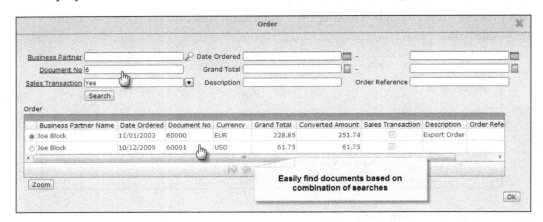

# Order and invoicing reports

The Compiere system provides standard templates of order reports that can be used to find the relevant document. Standard reports in the system include:

- Open orders
- Order transactions
- Invoicing transactions
- Invoice detail
- Daily, weekly, monthly, and quarterly invoice summary reports

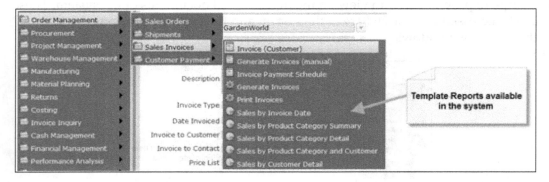

# User list reporting with or without querying

List reporting in Compiere is a standard feature that allows the end user the flexibility to create and manage their own reports. This feature can be accessed from any header or line level in the document. Although possible, sub reporting and custom reporting can become quite a challenge. In the Professional and Enterprise Edition, this can easily be overcome with business views or custom reports based on third-party reporting. Print formats are set up through the **Print Format** window.

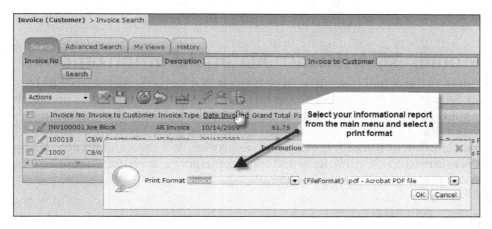

# Return Material Authorization (RMA)

The **Return Material Authorization (RMA)** process facilitates the process of customer returns. Non-customer returns must be captured through physical inventory adjustment, which is covered in the next chapter. Compiere workflow in the RMA process can be illustrated as follows:

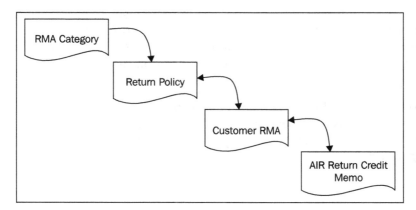

# RMA category

This allows the user to classify the reason for the return. It is not a required field for processing the return, but can be useful in analyzing reasons for returns.

# Return policies

These set the rules that determine when returns will be accepted. Return policies refer to a time-based indicator during which it is allowed to return stock items. Such return policies can be set per product or per product category.

# Customer RMA (Return Material Authorizations)

This refers to the actual items that the customer is returning. A customer RMA should be captured in reference to the original sales order or shipment on which it was sold. The system thus requires the RMA to be linked to the original sales document. RMA lines can also be linked to the sales order lines, either through manual selection or through the `copy from` process. It is essential that the customer RMA is returned to a locator for warehousing purposes. Inventory quantities are incremented once the document is completed.

# Return credit memo

Return credit memos can also be generated in batch or manually (as per the Generate Invoice process described above). Depending on the Sales Order type (i.e. POS order or Credit Order) a Return Credit Memo will be automatically created upon completion of the RMA document.

# Distribution runs

The system allows you to distribute products to your business partners based on a set minimum quantity or ratio of distribution. Distribution runs automatically create the Sales Orders associated with the distribution run. Orders will be created per business partner. Insufficient quantities to fulfill the distribution run rules will result in no orders being created (i.e where a minimum quantity is required for a run).

An example of this would be where available product is to be distributed to three business partners based on a 50:30:20 ratio. Following a distribution run process, the system would then generate three sales orders based on the product to those business partners.

# Sales processing accounting consequences

Sales processing transactions have flexible yet intricate accounting consequences. The order of set up is thus quite important in order to avoid future re-posting, or misallocations in the accounts. The major accounting elements affecting sales accounting would be Receivables, Revenue, Cost of Sales, and Inventory. The main rule in terms of Compiere accounting is that individual set-ups override grouping set-ups, and where there are no grouping set-ups, Compiere refers to the default accounts.

## Default accounts

The `Accounting Schema` determines the default accounts used. With the lack of appropriate detail set-up, the default accounts are referenced from the accounting schema.

## Receivables accounts

Receivables accounts are defaulted from their Business Partner Group Accounting set-up. Business partner groups determine the default receivables accounting, and individual customer accounting can be setup through individual business partner's customer accounting setup. Receivable value is calculated at document level.

## Revenue accounting

Revenue accounts are defaulted from their Product Category accounting set-up. Product Revenue accounts may also be individually edited. The revenue values are determined based on the invoice line values, and the posting is at line level.

## Cost of sales accounting

Product Categories determine the cost of sales accounting in the same manner as Revenue accounting. The value of such a cost of sale is determined by the product's valuation rule and time of shipment. For example, an average costing, standard costing, or last invoice price valuation rule may apply. Especially in a newly-installed environment, the valuation method must be closely monitored as transactional history may be lacking in the product cost queue.

In circumstances where there is a large volume of product lines, it is highly recommended that you manage revenue and cost of sale categories according to product categories and not by using individual product accounting rules. Care must be taken when product categories are changed, as changing the set-ups only affects new transactional processing and not historical transactions, unless explicitly re-posted in the system. Product Management is described in more detail in Chapter 4.

# Tax accounting

Based on the tax set-up, a tax due to you (debit) or owed by you (credit) is accounted for at the document level, but can be calculated based on individual line totals or document totals. A separate tab in the invoice window shows the tax that has been calculated.

# Summary of the accounts posting

The summary accounting for sales processing documents are as follows

| | Debit | Credit |
|---|---|---|
| Accounts Receivable Invoice | Receivable Asset (posted at the document level) | |
| | | Revenue (line level) based on the Business Partner or Business Partner Group |
| | | Tax Due (document level) |
| Accounts Receivable Credit Memo | | Receivable Asset (Document level) |
| | Revenue (line level) | |
| | Tax Due (document level) | |

Click on the **Posted** button per document indicating the detail of the accounts posting.

Here is a list of accounting entries for this sales invoice:

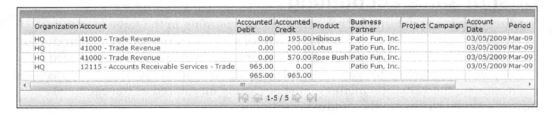

| Organization | Account | Accounted Debit | Accounted Credit | Product | Business Partner | Project | Campaign | Account Date | Period |
|---|---|---|---|---|---|---|---|---|---|
| HQ | 41000 - Trade Revenue | 0.00 | 195.00 | Hibiscus | Patio Fun, Inc. | | | 03/05/2009 | Mar-09 |
| HQ | 41000 - Trade Revenue | 0.00 | 200.00 | Lotus | Patio Fun, Inc. | | | 03/05/2009 | Mar-09 |
| HQ | 41000 - Trade Revenue | 0.00 | 570.00 | Rose Bush | Patio Fun, Inc. | | | 03/05/2009 | Mar-09 |
| HQ | 12115 - Accounts Receivable Services - Trade | 965.00 | 0.00 | | Patio Fun, Inc. | | | 03/05/2009 | Mar-09 |
| | | 965.00 | 965.00 | | | | | | |

1-5 / 5

Also refer to *Chapter 6. Compiere Financial Management* for more details on accounting processes.

# Sales regions

Business partners may be allocated to Sales Regions. If entered, sales region dimensions are intricately associated with document processing.

Sales regions are determined through the business partner locations tab. Sales Regions can be set up in a reporting hierarchy and linked to Sales representatives. Sales representatives are required information fields for orders, shipments, and invoices.

Sales Regions are set up through the Sales Region window

# Commissions

Document commission calculations are set up in the system to determine the value of commissions to be paid, for instance license or royalties to be paid based on periodic timing. Multiple commissions can be determined for the same order or invoice, and can be determined per sales representative at the document level, product, or product category level, or business partner grouping level. As mentioned, the basis of the calculation can be order, invoice, or receipt.

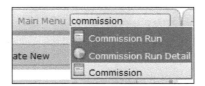

- **Commission window:** Set up commission calculations.

- **Commission run window**: The commission run process determines the payables values and documents to be generated from the commission calculations.

- **Commission run detail report**: This is a report for the commission detail.

# Summary

Sales processing is a complex process, and because Compiere is flexible in its processing there are many options available to the users, and it requires careful planning in the set-up and training of users of the system.

What we have learned in this chapter:

- How to define Business Partners, credit management, and how to enter leads
- Described the sales order to invoice process
- The meaning of different types of orders and their transactional implications
- How to generate sales invoices
- Reporting on Open Order, Invoice Inquiries, and Sales
- Described Returns Management and how commission calculations are facilitated
- Described the Accounting consequences of sales processing

In the next chapter, we will illustrate Product and Material management concepts.

# 4
# Product and Material Management

Products are an integral part of the ERP transactional process, and thus require a detailed explanation in the setup process, not only from the master data point of view but also for transactional processes. Material transactions are warehousing and physical inventory processes and controls.

We will therefore describe how Compiere handles Product and Materials Management. In this chapter we shall:

- Give you an overview of the concept of a product
- Show you how to set up price lists and discount schemas
- Give you an overview of materials management in Compiere, including warehousing, product quantities, and moving inventory
- Describe how to set up the replenishment of a product
- Give you an understanding of costing and accounting principles
- Give you an overview of the standard reports and business reporting views available

## The product definition

The concept of a product in Compiere is that it is something that you buy or sell and has a price. It would include:

- Inventory items (items that you store and track)
- Non-stock items (still items, but you do not store or track them)
- Services
- Resources
- Expense types

In addition to a product, Compiere allows for charges (account aliases), as well as customer assets on transactional lines.

**When to use a charge and not a product:** It's logical to use charges where a mere account entry is required and the many descriptions that a product requires are not required for the transaction. An example would be marketing or an admin expense.

**When to use a customer asset and not a product:** Customer assets are extended instances of a Compiere product. An example would be where a Desktop PC is sold or purchased and becomes an asset or equipment type that need to be tracked. Customer assets are therefore used for asset or equipment related business process information and are not covered as such in this book.

Products allow for many descriptive attributes in its master setup.

# Describing a product

Product information and features can be extended and described in Compiere in the following manner:

- **Basic Product Information**: Basic product information includes search key values, Descriptions, Unit of Measure, UPC, EAN. Critical for basic product information are Product categories, which group products into related products.

- **Product BOM (Bill of Material)**: More advanced products would include BOM kits that are made up of other products (referred to as BOM components).

- **Substitute / Related Products**: This refers to products that may be related to the product being searched for.

- **Product Replenishment**: This describes the rules of how a product would be replenished. This would, for instance, include minimum and maximum quantities to hold in stock.

- **Product Purchasing information**: This refers to the set-up around how a product is purchased—for instance the default vendor and the vendor's product code.

- **Product Locator**: Where products are currently located in the warehouse.

- **Product Business Partner**: This describes additional information used when products are purchased.

- **Product Price**: A product may have multiple price lists attached to it, and depending on the Business Partner or transactional document this can be defaulted as required.

- **Product Accounting**: This describes which standard account elements are to be used for a transactional document. Usually, similar products have the same accounting rules and as such the accounting for Product Categories would be setup and maintained, rather than individual product categories.

- **Product Unit of Measure conversions**: Where applicable, products may have conversions applicable to them — for instance converting a 6-pack quantity sold to an, each, quantity during purchasing.

- **Product Attributes**: Attribute sets allow you to further extend the product information into, for example, instance sets such as lots and serial numbers. Non-instance sets are also catered for, such as colour or size sets that can be used for searching the products.

# Setting up a Product

Prior to setting up a product, you should make sure that the following is set up:

- **Warehouse and Locators:** The system logic here is that a Product must be sold/delivered from somewhere within the organization. Make sure that you set up your warehouse and Locators first. Use virtual warehouse and locators where they are not physical.

- **Units of Measure:** Review the system standard units of measure and add your own units of measure if applicable.

- **Product Categories:** Define your groupings prior to setting up products since it will reduce data maintenance time.

- **Tax Categories:** Pre-define the applicable tax categories if they are product specific.

- **Price lists:** In order to use a product it must have a price which is set up through Price Lists (it includes sales and/or purchase price lists).

The above set-up is performed through the **Product Setup** menu items, which are grouped as follows in the main menu:

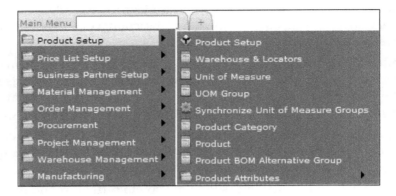

You start entering a product through the **Product** window:

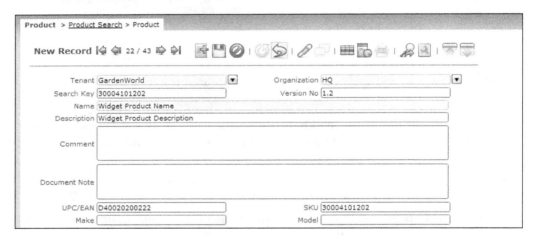

The additional Product Descriptions (listed above) are added through the following tabs in the Product window:

# Price Lists

In order for products to be used in the sales or purchasing cycle, they must have prices. A product can have the following three line prices set up:

- **List Price:** The list price before discounts of a product.
- **Standard Price:** The standard price of a product.
- **Limit Price:** The lowest price at which a product can be sold or purchased. Usually used by management as a pricing control limit for sales reps.

The product price information (in the context of the price list version) is accessed through the **Product | Price** window:

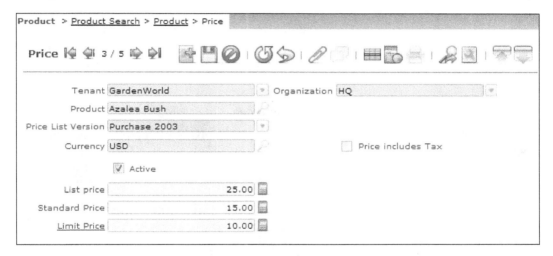

## Pricing logic flow

Price lists determine the price to be used in the context of the transaction (sales / purchase) and the chosen Business Partner. The basic logic for determining the price is as follows:

- A price list has a version, and the latest version of a price list is used during sales or purchasing (or both).
- If a Business Partner (customer or vendor) is assigned a Price list, then this Price List is used to determine the price for the transaction.
- If a Business Partner is not assigned a price list, then the Business Partner Group's defined price lists is used.

- If the Business Partner Groups' price list is not defined, then the default sales or purchase price list is used (this is indicated throught the **isDefault** checkbox in the price list window header).
- If a product is not assigned the relevant price list, an error is given and the user cannot continue.
- The system also considers that a price list is Tenant and Organization specific.

In terms of price discounting, a product can be assigned to a Discount Schema. In such a case, the following discount schema options are available:

- Price lists: This is the normal type of discount calculation, and is based on the price list-that is—a discount off the list price based on a distributor or reseller price list.
- Flat Percentage: This refers to a flat percentage discount arrangement.
- Quantity Discount Breaks: This discount schema refers to quantity breaks, where items purchased at different quantity levels attract more discount-for example,—100/10% or 1000/20%.

## Setting Up a Price List and version

As mentioned, a price list can have one or more versions, which are time based. This is set up as follows:

1. Enter a price list through the **Price List** window. Here, we enter a sales price list as follows:

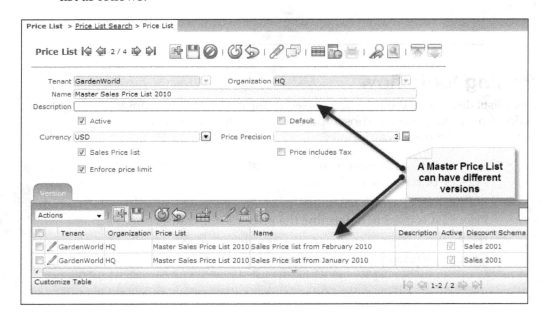

A price list may be set up to be inclusive of tax. In this case the accounts posting on the document is adjusted to reflect the inclusive tax accounting. Enforcing price limits ensures that the end-user cannot enter a price lower that the price lists, limit price for the product.

2. Create one or many price list versions through the **Price List | Version** tab, with the following options:

   - **Dicscount Schema:** This specifies the discount rules to be applied when creating or updating the price list.

   - **Base Price List:** This indicates a price list upon which to base the discount schema rules.

   - **Valid from date:** The price list will be used for new order or invoice transactions from this date. Transactions prior to this date will not be affected.

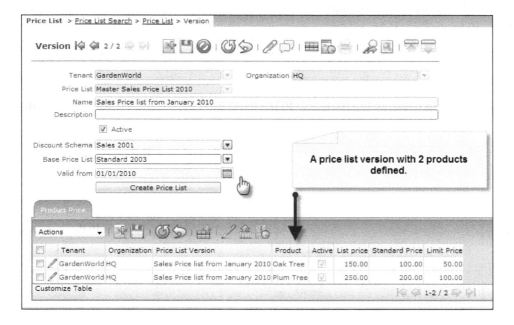

 A price list is either imported, manually entered, or updated based on another price list, through the discount schema.

# Illustrating a price list increase

To illustrate the process of a applying a price list increase, we will create a new price list version with a 10 percent increase on the existing version.

1. One enters the discount schema detail through the **Discount Schema** window. We will select a PriceList discount type, as the calculation will be based on the price list values:

2. The next step is to create the **Price List line** calculation paramaters for the discount schema:

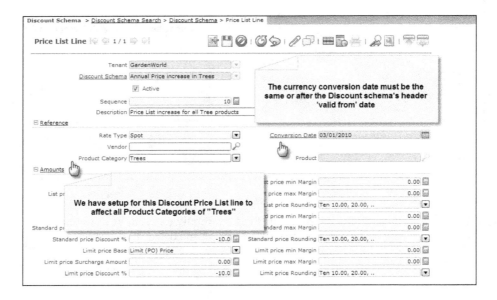

3. The pricing discount line for the increase is entered as follows:

   a. **Select the Price Base**: This defines which price base is affected (List, / Standard / Limit).

   b. **Enter the List price Discount:** A discount is normally entered as a positive, but because we are performing a price increase we enter a negative amount.

   c. **List Price Rounding option:** Compiere allows different rounding methods, and as illustrated we selected the Rounding to the nearest Ten (10,20,30) option, for pricing policy reasons.

4. Finally, we run the increase for the Price List version illustrated as follows:

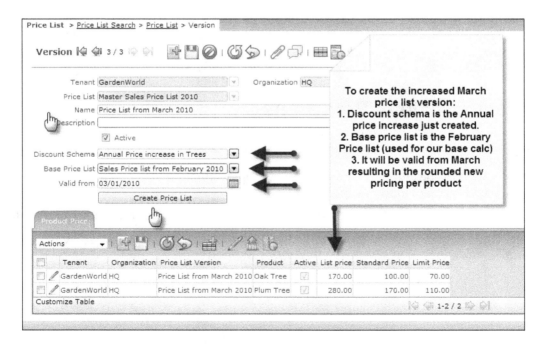

# Discount Breaks

Discount breaks are trade discounts applied through different quantity or value breaks/levels. Setting up a Discount Schema for discounts break based on a quantity sliding scale is entered through the **Discount Schema** window, as follows:

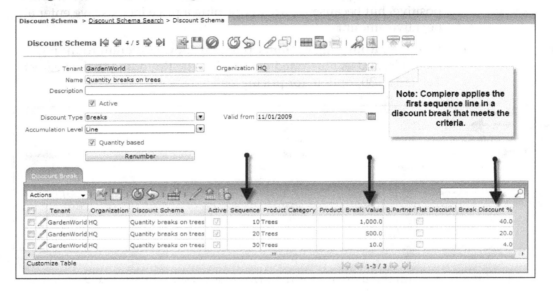

In a sliding scale discount break, Compiere applies the first discount break that meets the discount criteria, therefore for the example above, an order of **1000** or above would have a **40%** discount, **500-999** would have **20%** discount, an order of between **10** to **499** would have **4%** discount, and **0-9** would have **0%** discount.

# Pricing Decimal Precisions

Compiere allows for different pricing decimal precisions, which may be a requirement in the enterprise during different transaction types:

- **Unit of measure:** You can define pricing decimal precisions for accounting and cost calculation separately
- **Currency:** You can define pricing decimal precisions for accounting and cost calculation separately
- **Price List:** You can define the price precision

# Managing Products as Services

Service items are not treated as stock and are usually not purchased. Service items are managed as non-stocked items and have different accounting entry implications, by default. Service items are set up through the **Product** window as follows:

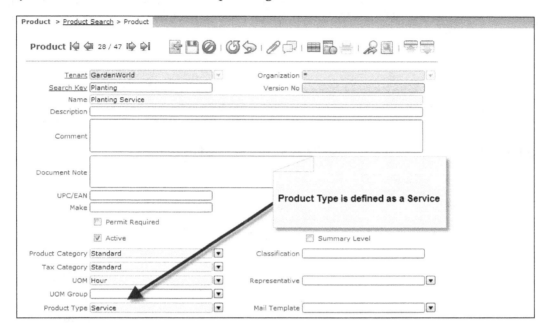

# Material Management

Material management within Compiere focuses on the physical side of storing and tracking items that are defined as being physically stocked. Central to this is the warehouse and its locators, into which and from where products are received, moved or shipped. In this section we will deal with Compiere standard functionality. An advanced Warehouse Management module with additional features is also available.

# Warehouse Overview

Warehouses belong to Organizations, and it is recommended that you have a one-to-one relationship if user security role access is an issue, because roles are organization specific. Warehouses can have multiple locators and one default locator is selected.

Warehouses and locators are set up through the **Warehouse & Locators** window:

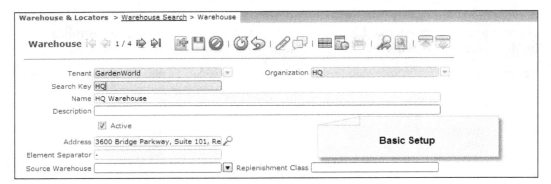

On the **Locator** tab, the warehouse locators are defined as follows:

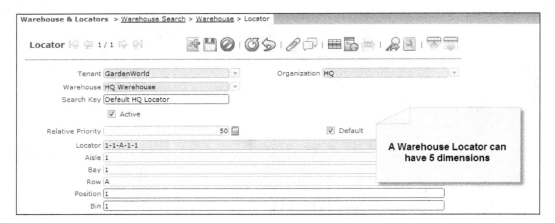

# Adjusting Product Quantities

Product quantities are adjusted through the **Physical Inventory** and **Internal Use** inventory windows. Physical Inventory adjustments are made during inventory counts or ad hoc manual inventory quantity adjustments, while Internal Use Inventory adjustments are made when items are expensed directly to a specific charge account:

# Physical Inventory Entry

Updating material item quantities is done through a physical inventory transaction. The book (system) values are updated to the applicable quantities counted, and the adjustment is passed to the product. An example of this would be for a product with a book quantity of 10 and a physical quantity of 20, where an adjustment of a positive quantity of 10 will be made. We shall demonstrate the process of quantity counting to perform a physical adjustment.

1. Preparing a quantity count is done through the **Physical Inventory** window:

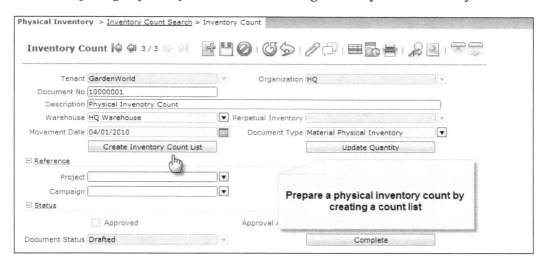

2. Create a count list of a Product Category:

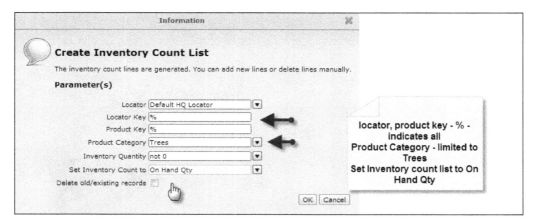

Note that you can also set the Inventory Count to Zero, which would indicate a blind count. The correct count quantities need to be updated for each product and location, and the Physical Inventory transaction completed to correct the stock quantities:

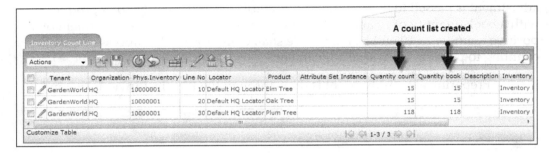

## Internal Use Inventory

Internal use inventory transactions are used for where products are written off or expensed, and not necessarily sold or shipped to customers.

The transaction window **Internal Use Inventory** is completed for this purpose:

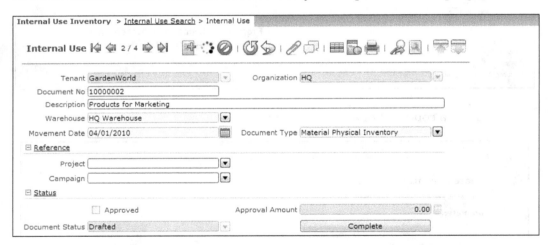

In the example illustrated below, the Product Quantity is charged to Marketing Expenses, based on its default Unit of Measure on the Internal Use Inventory line, as follows:

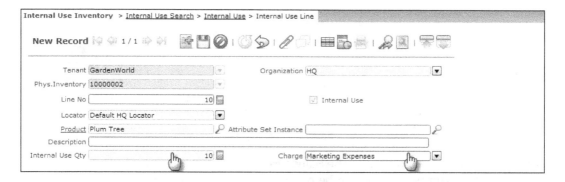

# Moving Inventory

There are two reasons for moving inventory:

- External: Material Shipments to Customers and Material Receipts from Vendors.
- Internal: Internal Warehouse movements within the warehouse.

 Movements between warehouses are also regarded as external and explicit. Material shipment and receipt documents need to be created as such (also refer to the Compiere concept or Counter Documents (not covered in this book) where, in such cases, explicit inter-organization counter transactions can be automatically created, if this has been set up).

# Material Shipments to Customers

Shipments are processed with reference to the Sales Order control document. We have previously explained that shipments occur based on the shipping rules defined in the Sales Order. Manual shipments are processed when the Standard Order sales order document type is used.

Processing a manual shipment (Generate Shipment from Order) is done through the **Generate Shipments (manual)** window:

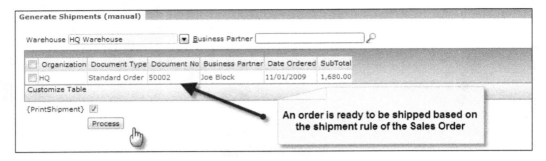

A shipment with lines linked to the Sales Order lines will be created for this customer. This shipment can then be printed as a delivery note:

The default printed shipment document will look like the example shown in the following screenshot:

# Material Receipts from Vendors

Material Receipt transactions adjust product quantities by entering inventory into the system. Materials must be received into a warehouse, and during this process they may not need a price. Ultimately, product Material Receipts need to be matched against Purchase Orders and Accounts Payable(AP) Invoices. Costing entries are not adjusted until the Material Receipts are matched to accounts payable invoices.

Material Receipt transactions are processed through the **Material Receipt** window as follows:

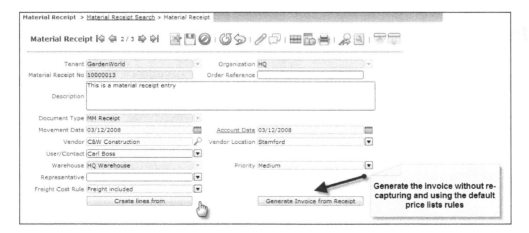

The **Create lines from** button provides the ability to create receipt lines from another document and create an automatic link to the originating document:

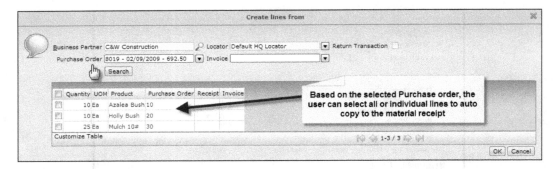

Material Receipt Lines created are based on this information:

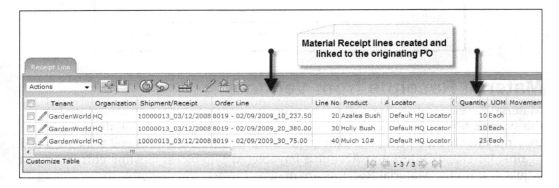

Once the Material Receipt line is completed, the product items are adjusted to the warehouse and locator as specified for each line.

# Internal Inventory Move

Inventory move transactions facilitate the internal movement of products between locators in a warehouse. These are entered through the **Inventory Move** window:

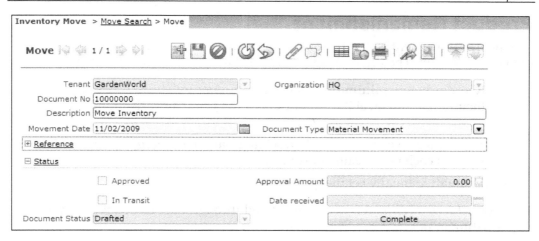

The **Inventory Move Lines** tab indicates the product line information:

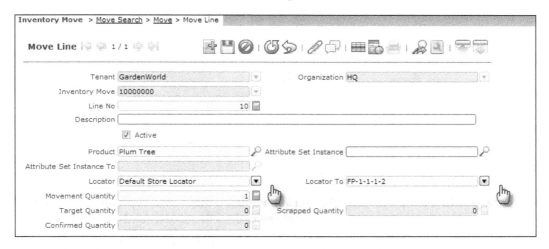

Here, a product is moved from a **Default Store Locator** to an **FP-1-1-1-2** locator. On completion of this document, the material transaction is created to move the items from one locator to the other.

# Product Replenishment

Product replenishment is done through pre-defined criteria, during the replenishment run. The pre-defined criteria in Compiere are the following:

- **Reorder below minimum level:** Product items will be re-ordered to their maximum level if their stock on hand goes below the minimum quantity level.

- **Maintain Maximum level:** Product items are re-ordered to their maximum level on each replenishment run.

- **Manual:** Manually set the quantity to order.

The product replenishment criteria are defined through the **Product window > Replenishment** tab:

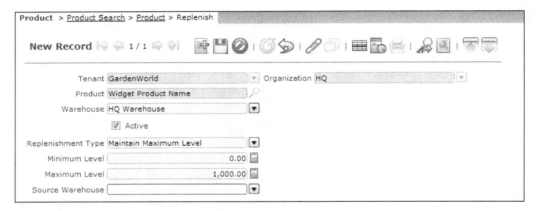

Once the product's replenishment criteria have been defined, a replenishment run creates a replenishment report, and purchase orders to subsequently be raised.

The **Stock Replenishment report** menu item is selected as follows, in order to run the report and create the inventory move, purchase order, or requisition transaction:

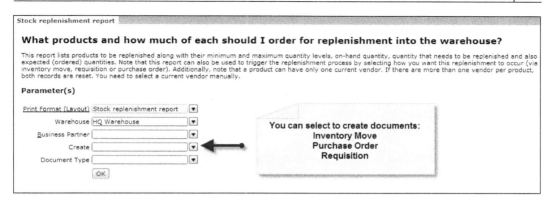

The stock replenishment report would look something like the example shown in the following screenshot:

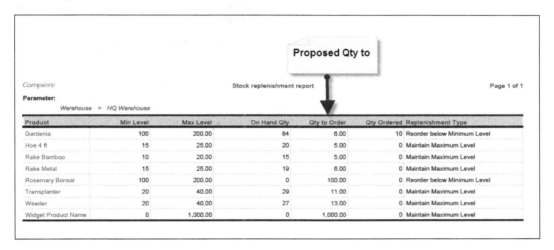

The user is by no means bound to the proposed replenishment quantity, and should the user choose to create a Replenishment document (Inventory Move, Purchase Order, or Requisition) the quantities can be changed because the document would be initially created in a drafted state.

# Product Costing and Accounting

Products can be valued through various costing methods, including Average Invoice, Last PO, Last Invoice, Standard Costing, FiFo, LiFO, and Average PO. A Product's costing is only updated based on the matching process between Purchase Orders and/or Material Receipt and/or Accounts Payable Invoices, and depending on which costing method is required it will be calculated accordingly. A Purchase Order is not required for the Average Invoice, Last Invoice, Fifo, and Lifo costing methods.

A typical example of the Average Invoice costing method to be applied would mean that an AP Invoice has been matched to a material receipt for that product item. The Cost of Goods Sold accounting post entry value (in the **Shipment (Customer)** transaction) is thus dependent upon this product's cost having been created before the product has been sold.

Different costing methods may be used for different product categories. This is set up through the `Product` **Category | Accounting** window:

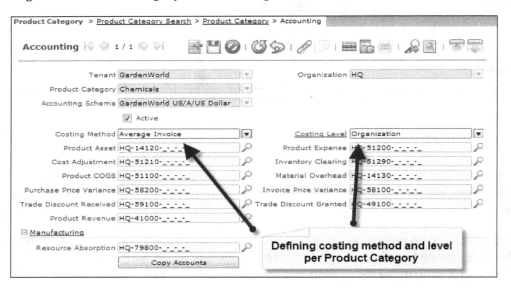

Defining costing method and level per Product Category

It is important to note that the Compiere system will give Posting Errors where a product is being used on a document but no costs have been defined (as a result of proper matching not being achieved, for instance).

You can display a product's costs through the **Product Costs** window:

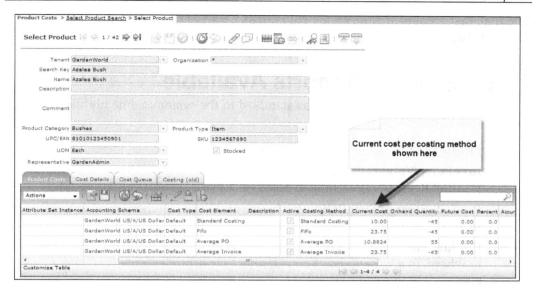

# Typical Accounting of product warehouse transactions

The normal accounting of a product using its current cost per costing method applicable would be as follows:

|  | Debit | Credit |
|---|---|---|
| Material Receipt into warehouse | Product Asset | |
|  | | Not Invoiced Liability |
| Accounts Payable Invoice | Not Invoiced Liability | |
|  | | Accounts Payable Liability |
| Material Shipment to customer | Cost of Goods Sold Expense | |
|  | | Product Asset |
| Internal use Inventory | Charge Expense | |
|  | | Product Asset |
| Physical Inventory (inventory difference – qty reduced) | Inventory Shrinkage | |
|  | | Product Asset |
| Inventory Move | Product Asset | |
|  | | Product Asset |

The matched accounting entries are covered as a part of the purchasing process, in the next chapter.

# Basic Product Reports Available

Compiere provides various reports as standard in the system. Some highlighted reports would include:

- **Product list:** A list of the products in the system.
- **Inventory Valuation report:** This is a report showing the valuation of product items per warehouse, based on a price list and valuation date.
- **Product Storage Detail:** By warehouse and locator, where products are stored, and their relevant quantities.
- **Product movement detail:** What products were moved, from where and to where, in a warehouse. You can select these movements based on a specific movement type.
- **Material Receipt Details:** Details of a material receipt.
- **Receipts not matched to invoices:** List of receipts not matched to invoices.
- **Shipment Details:** Details of a shipment to a customer.

# Product Info Window

The **Product Info** window is a handy quick reference to get an overview of a product's pricing and quantity availability per warehouse.

The **Product Info** window is accessed through the **View | Product Info** menu item:

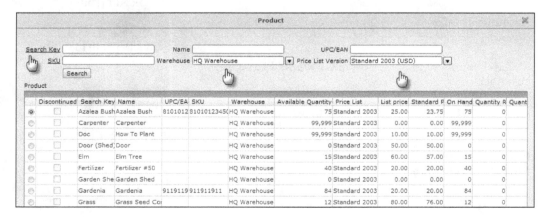

You can search based on search key, name, UPC/EAN, SKU and warehouse. A product must have a price list defined in order to be viewed in this window.

# Summary

We covered the following in this chapter:

- The basic characteristics of a product, and how to set up a product item
- How to set up and use price lists and discount schemas
- Material management principles, including how to create a warehouse, locators, and how to facilitate:
  - ° Product Quantity management including physical inventory and internal use inventory
  - ° Material Receipts into the warehouse
  - ° Material Shipments out of the warehouse
  - ° Inventory moves within the warehouse
- Description of the basic principle of product replenishment.
- Overview of costing methods and accounting principles
- Overview of basic reports available and the info view

In the next chapter, we will illustrate the procurement process.

# 5
# Procurement Management

Procurement management is the process of managing the acquisition of goods, expense items, and services from an organization's suppliers (in Compiere, these suppliers are referred to as Vendors).

We will review how Compiere handles Procurement Management in this chapter, and shall:

- Give you an overview of the business flows in the Procurement transaction process
- Illustrate how Requisitions are captured and converted to Purchase Orders
- Show you how Purchase Orders are matched to Accounts Payable invoices
- Create Material Receipts from Purchase Orders or Invoices
- Match documents in the Procurement cycle
- Give you an overview of the accounting principles
- Explain in detail the standard reports available in the system

# The Procurement flow

In following best practice design, Compiere facilitates the Procurement flow as shown follows:

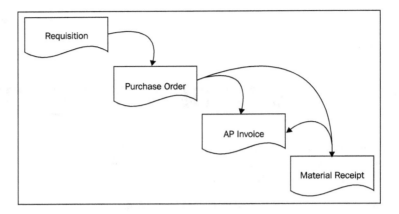

The specific entry point into the Procurement cycle is very flexible and documents do not initially have to link to each other. In effect, you do not require a Purchase Order to have an Accounts Payable (AP) Invoice or a Material Receipt. How the procurement cycle transactional document flow is linked and implemented for an organization is entirely flexible. In this process however, the Purchase Order is the control document and it is a best practice that as a minimum a Purchase Order always be created to start the procurement cycle, because this is the typical legal instruction required by a Vendor in order to commence a procurement transaction.

The transaction windows for this process in Compiere are found under the **Procurement** menu item:

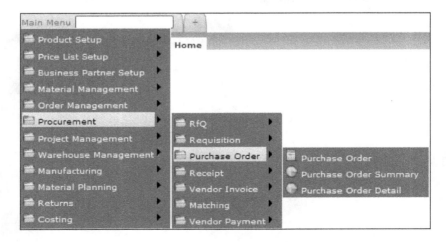

Processing Products setup as items (stocked or non-stocked) and setting up Products as service items is exactly the same. The difference is that the quantity on hand cannot be tracked for such items.

# Requisition documents

A Requisition is an organization's internal document that is used by staff or departments for procurement's pre-approval prior to the issue of a Purchase Order to a Vendor. Based on a parameter such as the actual required date, a Purchase Order is then generated. Separate Purchase Orders are created per the line Product's Purchasing Business Partners and where applicable these required Purchase Orders can be selected to be consolidated into one document.

A Requisition is entered through the menu **Procurement > Requisition > Requisition** window. The basic information required would be the employee, a description, date required, warehouse, and applicable price list:

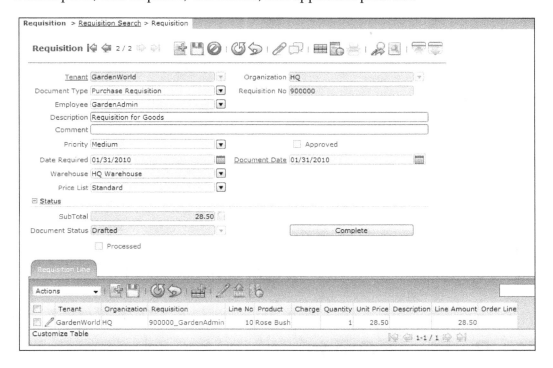

In order to generate a Purchase Order from the captured Requisition, use the **Procurement > Requisition > Generate PO from Requisition** process:

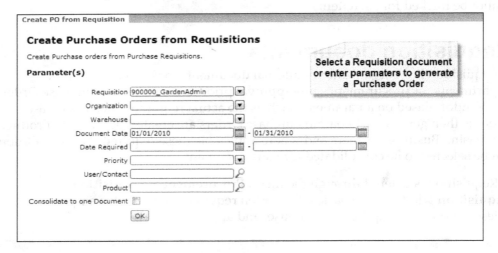

Once it has run, the Purchase Order(s) generated are listed:

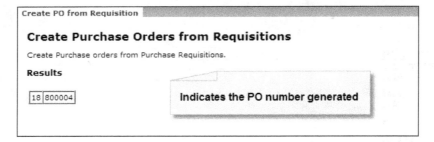

**Try setting up a Requisition approval workflow.**

A good practice would be to set up a workflow for the approval of Requisitions prior to the Purchase Orders being generated. We cover the workflow process in *Chapter 7, Advanced Aspects*.

# The Purchase Order

Purchase Orders are the commercial control document within the Procurement cycle and are generally accepted as indicating the organization's contractual obligation with a Vendor for the supply of goods or services, and the subsequent payment for these goods or services. It is, however, not a Compiere system-required document within the Procurement cycle.

The system provides various sources from which Purchase Orders can be automatically generated from:

- **Replenishment Run:** After an inventory replenishment run, Purchase Orders can be created.

- **From Sales Orders:** The system provides the ability to create Purchase Orders from Sales Orders.

- **From Requisitions:** As described above, Purchase Orders can be generated from requisitions.

- **From Projects:** Purchase Orders can be created from Projects.

- **From Works Orders:** Purchase Orders can be created from Works Orders.

# Capturing the Purchase Order

Firstly, Purchase Order header information is entered into the **Purchase Order** window. The information that would be required are the Organization, Date Ordered, Vendor, Vendor location, Warehouse, Price List, and Representative:

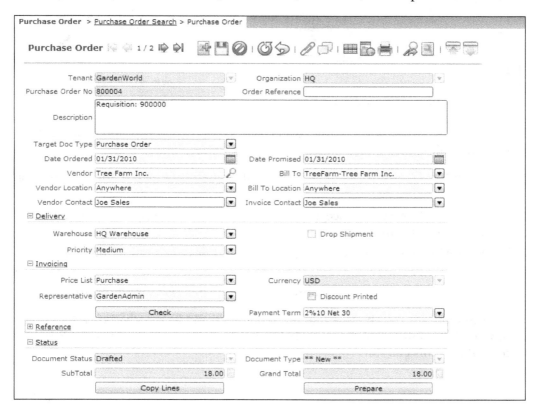

Secondly, purchase line level information is entered in the **PO Lines** tab. This would include the Product or Charge, Quantity required, and Price:

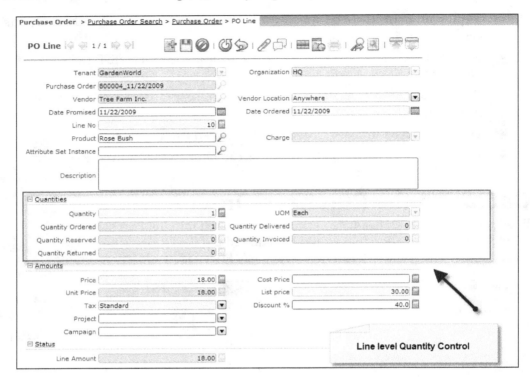

On the Purchase Order line, the line level Order Quantity controls are facilitated through the following:

- **Quantity / Quantity Ordered:** This is the Quantity Entered and Ordered for the line

- **Quantity Reserved:** Once an order has been created a product's quantity is reserved for purchase

- **Quantity Delivered: A** material receipt updates the quantity delivered, and **Quantity Reserved** is reduced

- **Quantity Invoiced:** The quantity invoiced increases as invoices are created

The requirement for the above is that documents should be matched on a line-by-line basis. We will review the Matching Purchase order to Invoice and Material Receipt process later in this chapter.

**Closing a Purchase Order:**
Once a Purchase Order has been closed, the **Quantity Reserved** is reset to zero. The purchase order cannot be used again.

# Material Receipt

A Material Receipt is the system transaction document that updates quantities in inventory, and pertains to a warehouse location. It may or may not link to a Purchase Order, depending on the organization's business rules. Material receipts link to Purchase Orders and can be created from a Purchase Order without having to re-enter all of the lines. Once entered, the related Accounts Payable (AP) Invoice can be system-generated (created and linked) without having to re-enter all of the lines again. This not only speeds up the capturing process, but also ensures consistency in the matching at document line level.

## Capturing the Material Receipt

First, we create a Material Receipt header through the **Material Receipt** window. In this example, we capture the Vendor, Movement Date, Warehouse, and then we create lines from a created Purchase Order:

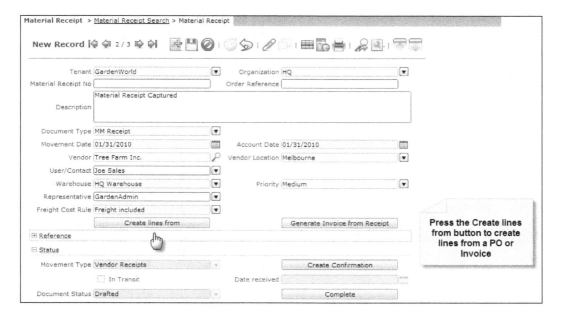

After clicking on the **Create Lines From** button in the **Material Receipt window,** the user must select the Purchase Order and the applicable lines that must be created:

A Material Receipt line must always be linked to a warehouse locator as follows:

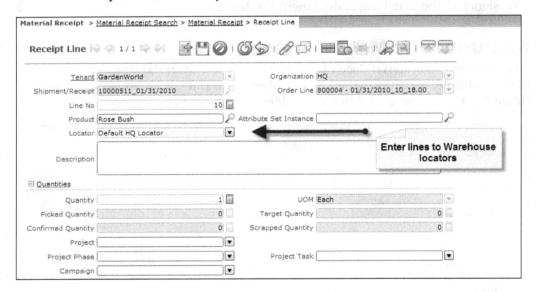

 An additional available process for Material Receipts is the Confirmation transaction. The Confirmation step provides an approval check to confirm the received quantities prior to making the quantities finally available in inventory. By enabling the **Ship/Receipt confirmation** in the document type window, this confirmation step will be a required check.

# Accounts Payable (AP) invoice

AP invoices increase the purchasing accounting liability, and add the value (cost price) to the transaction. AP invoices can be created from Purchase Orders or Material Receipts. Also, if the AP invoice and supplier's delivery note are the same document, the Material Receipt can be generated from the AP invoice without having to re-capture any data.

AP invoices are linked to purchase price lists, and therefore pricing can be pre-determined by having a product item's price lists managed within the system.

# Capturing the AP invoice

An AP invoice (or AP Credit Memo) is a document type created in the **Invoice (Vendor)** window. Capturing an AP invoice requires a Vendor Invoice number, date, Vendor, Vendor Location, Price List, and Representative:

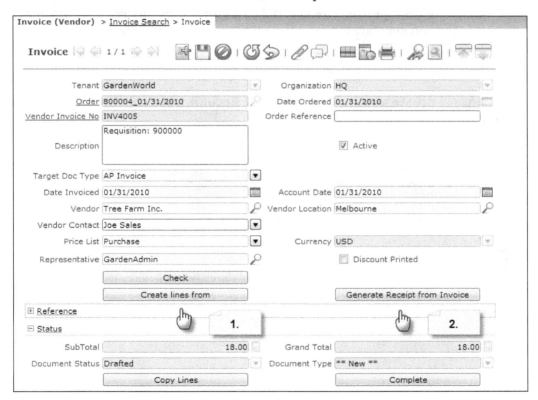

Once the basic information has been entered, you may capture the lines manually or, if the document is linked to a Purchase Order or Material Receipt, automatically create the invoice lines, as follows:

1. **Create Lines from**: Create the invoice document lines from Purchase Orders or Material Receipts:

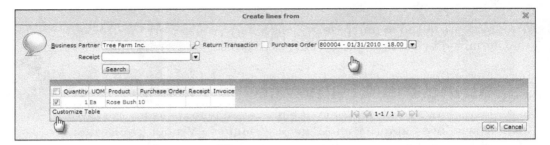

2. **Generate Receipt from Invoice**: If the receipt and the invoice are the same, the user can generate the receipt from the invoice automatically.

>  The Material Receipt is generated, but to a drafted state. You will have to confirm the details of the Material Receipt, and complete the documents, manually.

# Invoices for expense items (charges)

Invoices for expenses are entered at the line-level, with reference to charges and not products. Charges will post directly to the accounting tables as debit expenses on an AP invoice document type. On the **Invoice Line** tab, select the **Charge** field and not the product, as follows:

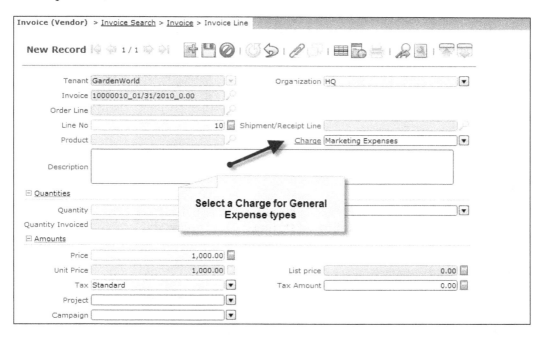

# Matching the Purchase Order, Receipt, and Invoice

Matching the Purchase Order, Material Receipt, and AP Invoice is a required process where product items are stocked and accurate information is required in terms of Quantities Ordered versus Delivered versus Invoiced, as well as for Product Costing Calculations and accounting. Because the Purchase Order is the control document, this is where the control of the respective statuses is displayed.

It is highly recommended that documents are matched automatically during processing by using the **create from** and **generate** process buttons in the Material Receipt and AP Invoice header documents.

The matching tabs are displayed by selecting the **Advanced Tabs** checkbox in the **Preferences** window:

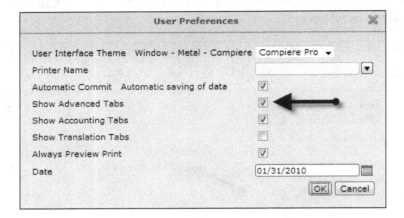

On the bottom of the invoice (vendor) window, the matching tabs, from where applicable documents can be followed through, are displayed:

After a document has been matched, a matching transaction is created. This can be found through the **Matched Invoices** window:

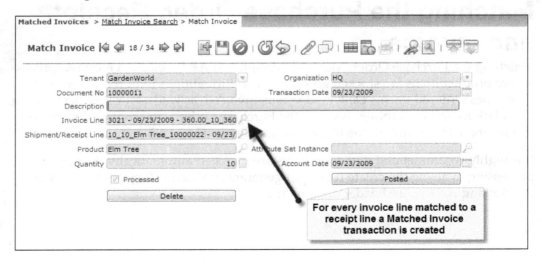

A transaction for matched Purchase Orders is created. This can be accessed through the **Matched Purchase Orders** window:

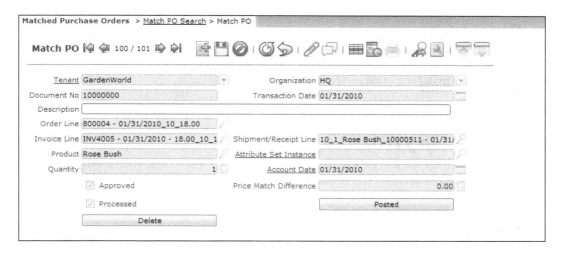

# Manually matching lines

Compiere provides a window that can be used to manually match the PO, Material Receipt, and AP Invoice. This transaction is accessed through the **Matching-PO-Receipt-Invoice** window, in which you can select where to match from and to (i.e. invoice to receipt), and select the appropriate lines to match, as follows:

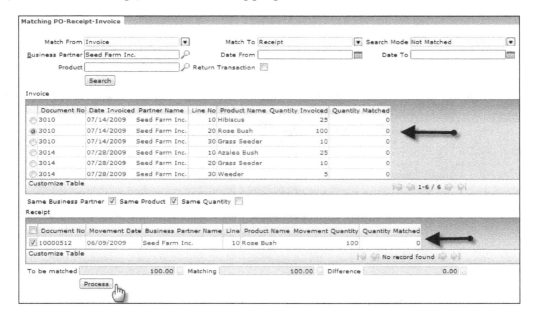

If the quantities match, then clicking on the **Process** button will generate the appropriate **Matched Invoices** transaction as described above.

Not following matching disciplines (i.e. generate from or manual) in the system can lead to problematic and large variance and clearance accounts. Also, for product cost element calculations to work, matching must be applied in most circumstances.

# Vendor payments

Compiere provides for the processing of payments for Vendor invoices either in batch or via a manual selection process.

# Batch processing

Selecting invoices using batch-based criteria is done through the **Payment Selection** window. Enter a name and bank account for the batch, and then create payment selection lines as follows:

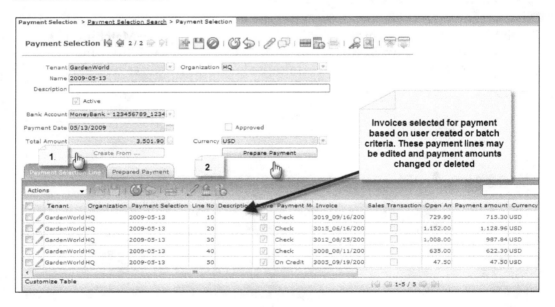

1. Invoices for **Payment Selection Lines** are created in batch by clicking on the **Create From** button selection criteria:

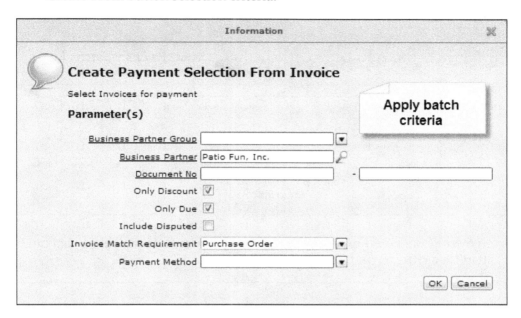

2. If the user clicks on the **Prepare Payment** button, the Compiere system summarizes the invoices for payment into Payments to be generated. This is seen through the **Prepared Payments** tab. Herewith two payments are thus created:

Finally, to print the payments and remittance advice, select the payment batch through the **Payment Print/Export** menu item and window:

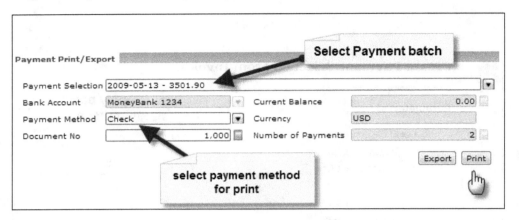

The Payment print would produce the following payment document (which can be formatted for a check layout or payment list):

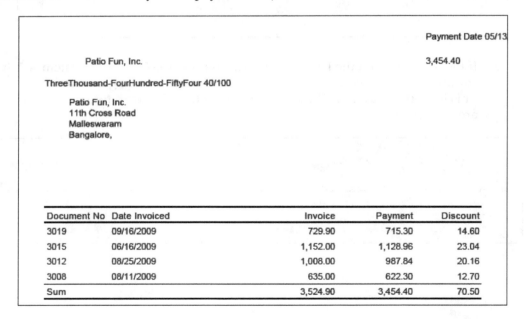

| Document No | Date Invoiced | Invoice | Payment | Discount |
|---|---|---|---|---|
| 3019 | 09/16/2009 | 729.90 | 715.30 | 14.60 |
| 3015 | 06/16/2009 | 1,152.00 | 1,128.96 | 23.04 |
| 3012 | 08/25/2009 | 1,008.00 | 987.84 | 20.16 |
| 3008 | 08/11/2009 | 635.00 | 622.30 | 12.70 |
| Sum | | 3,524.90 | 3,454.40 | 70.50 |

# Manual selection of invoices for payment

The manual selection of invoices for payment is handled through the **Payment Selection (Manual)** menu item and window. Select your **Bank Account** and **Business Partner,** and the system will display the invoices due for payment by clicking on the **Search** button:

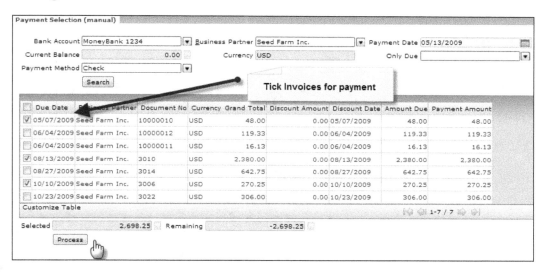

In the above window, the user selects the invoices due for payment, and then clicks the **Process** button, from where the process for printing the payments and remittance advices as described above is started.

In both batch selection and manual processing of the invoice, generated payments are automatically allocated for open item management purposes. This process is covered in more detail in *Chapter 6, Compiere Financial Management.*

# Returns to vendors

Returns to vendors have a basic process flow as follows, and processing is very similar to the processing of documents already mentioned above. The overview of the process is as follows:

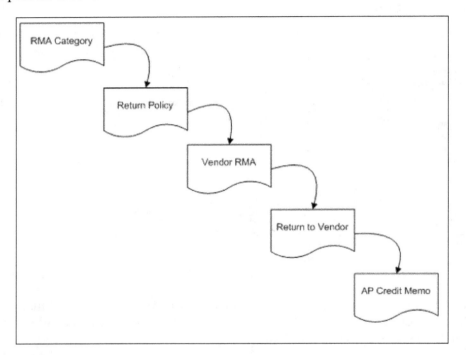

- **RMA Category:** A basic description of the **Return Material Authorization (RMA)** categories, i.e. Damaged goods.

- **Return Policy:** Defines the number in days within which returns are allowed, per product or per product category.

- **Vendor RMA:** This is required in an internal document to record the details of the authorization for a return to a vendor. It can be used for record keeping or as part of an internal or external approval workflow. In its simplest form it is the commercial opposite of a Purchase Order.

- **Return to Vendor:** This is the transactional document that records the quantities to return to the vendor from the warehouse. This is the opposite of a Material Receipt.

- **Accounts Payable (AP) Credit Memo:** Once a Return to Vendor document has been completed, a credit note can be generated, thus adding a value to the transaction. This is the opposite of an Accounts Payable (AP) Invoice.

# Compiere accounting for Procurement

Procurement documents have intricate accounting consequences. The order of set-up is thus quite important in order to avoid incorrect posting or misallocations in the accounting ledgers. The major accounting elements affecting Procurement accounting are Payables, Inventory, Variances, and Charges. The main rule in terms of Compiere accounting is that individual set-ups override Product Category or Business Partner Grouping set-ups, and where there are no grouping set-ups it refers to the default accounts:

- **Default accounts:** The Accounting Schema determines the default accounts used. When generating new categories or performing accounting set-up, the default accounts are referenced from the accounting schema.

- **Payables accounts:** Payables accounts are initially set up through the Business Partner Groups. Business Partner Groups determine the default payables accounting, and individual vendor accounting can be set up through individual business partner accounting.

- **Inventory and Variance accounting:** Product categories post to categorized inventory accounts, and products individually post per their individual product accounting set-up. Matching variance values are determined according to the invoice line values, and the posting is at line level.

- **Charge accounting:** Expense invoices' charges on AP invoices post to the relevant account indicated for such a charge.

Summary accounting of the accounting consequences

An accounts payable invoice posts at the invoice line level. When a Product is entered on the line, the following accounting will apply:

| Debit / Credit | Detail |
|---|---|
| DR Product Inventory Clearing (line level) | This is a debit entry that is made to the product inventory account for each invoice price line. |
| DR Tax Credit (document level) | Tax credit (receivable) at the document level |
| CR Payable (document level) | This is a Business Partner booking creating a credit to the Payables (Vendor) liability account per line. |

When an Accounts Payable Invoice is captured with a Charge selected on the line, the following accounting will apply:

| Debit / Credit | Detail |
|---|---|
| DR Charge Account (line level) | Per the charge accounting, a debit is made to the charge expense account. |
| DR Tax Credit (document level) | Tax credit (receivable) at the document level |
| CR Payable (document level) | Per the Business Partner accounting, this creates a credit to the Payables(Vendor) liability account. |

Generally, a Material Receipt will have the following accounts postings:

| Debit / Credit | Detail |
|---|---|
| DR Product Asset | Per line, a debit entry is made to the Product Asset account at the product's current cost |
| CR Not Invoiced Receipts | Per the Business Partner Group accounting, this creates a credit to the Not Invoiced Receipts account. The Not invoiced Receipts accounts is cleared through the invoice matching entry. |

The Matched Invoice accounts posting generates the following :

| Debit / Credit | Detail |
|---|---|
| DR Not Invoiced Receipts | Per the Business Partner Group accounting, this creates a debit to the Not Invoiced Receipts account at the product's current cost. |
| CR Product Inventory Clearing | Per line, a credit entry is made to the product inventory account at the product's invoice price. |
| DR / CR Invoice Price Variance | Based on the Standard Costing rule, the difference between an invoice price and a product's current cost is passed as a debit or credit variance entry based on the product accounting setup. DR – if the invoice price is more than the current cost. CR – if the invoice price is less than the current cost. |

Should the costing rule of Average PO or Last PO price be required, the Matched Purchase Order produces the following accounting entry:

| Debit / Credit | Detail |
|---|---|
| DR / CR  Purchase Price Variance | Based on the difference between the Purchase Order value and the product's current cost, a debit or credit variance entry is passed, based on the product accounting setup. |
| | DR – if the Purchase Order price is more than the current cost. |
| | CR – if the Purchase Order price is less than the current cost. |
| DR / CR Purchase Price Variance Offset | This is a contra variance account |

In order to view the document's accounting consequences, click on the **posted** button for a document indicating the details of the accounts posting.

An example of the of an Accounts Payable (AP) invoice is as follows:

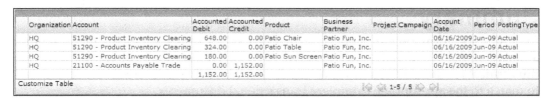

| Organization | Account | Accounted Debit | Accounted Credit | Product | Business Partner | Project | Campaign | Account Date | Period | PostingType |
|---|---|---|---|---|---|---|---|---|---|---|
| HQ | 51290 - Product Inventory Clearing | 648.00 | 0.00 | Patio Chair | Patio Fun, Inc. | | | 06/16/2009 | Jun-09 | Actual |
| HQ | 51290 - Product Inventory Clearing | 324.00 | 0.00 | Patio Table | Patio Fun, Inc. | | | 06/16/2009 | Jun-09 | Actual |
| HQ | 51290 - Product Inventory Clearing | 180.00 | 0.00 | Patio Sun Screen | Patio Fun, Inc. | | | 06/16/2009 | Jun-09 | Actual |
| HQ | 21100 - Accounts Payable Trade | 0.00 | 1,152.00 | | Patio Fun, Inc. | | | 06/16/2009 | Jun-09 | Actual |
| | | 1,152.00 | 1,152.00 | | | | | | | |

Customize Table   1-5 / 5

# Procurement reports

Predefined reports are available in the system as standard within the procurement flow. These are as follows:

- **Open Requisitions report**: A report of all open requisitions in the system.
- **Open Orders report**: A report of all open Purchase Orders in the system. The Sales and Purchasing reports are generated from the same menu item. Refer to *Chapter 3, Customers and Sales Process.*
- **Purchase Orders summary**: A list of all purchase orders for a period in time.

- **Purchase Order detail**: Shows line-level detail of what products or services were purchased, and from where.
- **Material Receipts detail**: Shows line-level detail of what products or services were received.
- **Material Receipts not matched**: This reports details of the material receipts that are not matched to invoices.
- **Purchases by vendor detail**: Report showing which items were purchased, per vendor.
- **Purchases by invoice date**: Showing the purchases by invoice date selection.
- **Purchases by Product Category summary**: Report selection by Product Category.
- **Purchases by Product Category and vendor**: Report selection by Category and Vendor.
- **Compiere Enterprise Edition:** Available Compiere executive dashboards are of the following types:
  - Top 5 expenditures
  - Top 5 vendors
  - Purchases by region
  - Purchases by period
  - Purchases by period and representative

# Summary

In its simplest form, procurement is the processing of a delivery note (material receipt) and Accounts Payable (AP) Invoice, where the process becomes more complex. It is thus critical for the enterprise to map out the steps in their procurement process and to match to the appropriate Compiere transactional documents.

We have covered the following in this chapter:

- The process flow of the Procurement cycle within the Compiere system
- Described the main transaction documents within the procurement cycle, namely Requisition, Purchase Order, Material Receipt, and Accounts Payable Invoices
- Given an overview of the returns to vendor process
- Describe the accounting entries of the various procurement documents
- Listed the various reports in the procurement process

In the next chapter we will illustrate the applicable processes involved in Financial Management and Accounting.

# 6
# Compiere Financial Management

In a world measured by money, all business processes materialize as an event in the accounting department. As a minimum, a budget is allocated to processes, or the financial impact of a process needs to be recorded in an Information System (ERP). The true power of Compiere is reflected in the intricate, flexible, and integrated information layers of its accounting engine. In the previous chapters we have described the sales cycle, inventory and purchasing cycle, and the accounting consequences of the relevant documents. In this chapter we explain the accounting and financial aspects of the system, and will do the following:

- Give you an overview of the Compiere accounting terminology
- Explain how accounting entries are derived
- Show you the accounting set-up required
- Explain open item management and the reconciliation of Accounts Receivable and Accounts Payable ledgers
- Explain cash management reconciliation
- Show you how to follow up on unposted documents
- Give you an overview of, and set up the financial reporting

In this chapter, we assume that you have a basic knowledge of accounting, and a working knowledge of Compiere List Reporting functionality.

# Accounting terminology in Compiere

In essence, Compiere adheres to the rule that accounting entries are at the lowest level, and an applicable document will have a derived accounting entry (fact). In order for you to understand the accounting process, there are Compiere accounting terms that must be clarified:

- **Accounting schema:** The set-up of the accounting schema defines the default rules and accounts of the Compiere tenant instance.

- **Account elements:** This refers to the natural account (debit or credit) used for the accounting balance entry (fact) posting. The posting to such elements can be actual, budget, or statistical. A chart of accounts is the listing of the account elements of the enterprise, which includes the account elements that make up the assets, liability, revenue, and expense accounts.

- **Accounting fact:** This refers to the accounting posting entry.

- **Account combination:** The account combination is a shortened reference (alias) to the accounting information dimension. For instance, telephone may refer to an account combination which would look like HQ-11100-Telephone-_-_-_.

- **Trail balance:** A trail balance report indicates the debit or credit balances of the list of accounts.

- **Financial report:** A financial report is run by a user and includes rows and columns that make up, for instance, Profit/Loss statement and balance sheet (financial position) reports.

- **Re-posting accounts:** This describes the action of re-posting a transaction document based on a new rule or default account that changed.

- **Unposted document:** These are documents that are entered and may be in a drafted or completed state, but for which the accounting engine has not generated the accounting entry. This could be due to a closed period, or because the accounting processor is not yet run.

- **Document date versus Accounting date:** Compiere documents usually allow for a document date and a separate accounting date field to be used for the accounting entry.

- **Calendar year and period:** While a transaction will fall into a period, the calendar period is used for control and reporting purposes. There is no end of period or roll-over process as such in Compiere.

# Understanding the accounting entry

In essence, the accounting entry principle can be illustrated as follows:

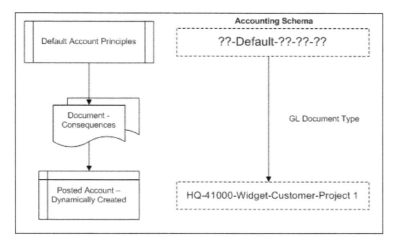

The figure above describes that the final accounting entry is created from the accounting schema rules and the default accounts, through the particular document type, which determines the accounting principle. Thus, an Accounts Receivable invoice will have a particular accounting entry that is different from, say, a Shipment or Accounts Payable document. The processes around these documents and their accounting entries have been described, when looking at the previous chapters in their respective business cycles.

The accounting processing engine of Compiere is separate from the document processing engine. Accounting entries are posted in the background, as a separate process.

Because of the decoupled accounting engine, Compiere allows for multiple currencies, multiple calendars, multiple charts of account (for instance accounting versus tax reporting), multiple GAAP (accrual and cost), and multiple costing methods, in the same instance (Tenant based). It also allows for the re-posting of documents based on new rules or default accounts.

Because accounting set-ups are an integral requirement of the initial system set-up, we have described the set-up of the Accounting Schema and Account Elements in detail, in Chapter 2.

# Accounting setup flow

The recommended sequence of set-up of Compiere accounting can be illustrated as follows:

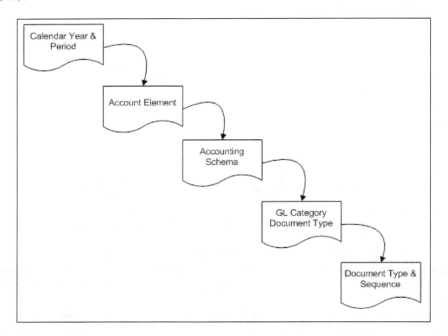

# Calendar year and period

Depending on the requirements of the enterprise, the calendar year and period setup requires the definition of the calendar year (for instance 2010, 2011, or 2012) as well as the periods for that year (the financial reporting months).

The default set-up is illustrated as follows, through the **Calendar Year and Period** menu item:

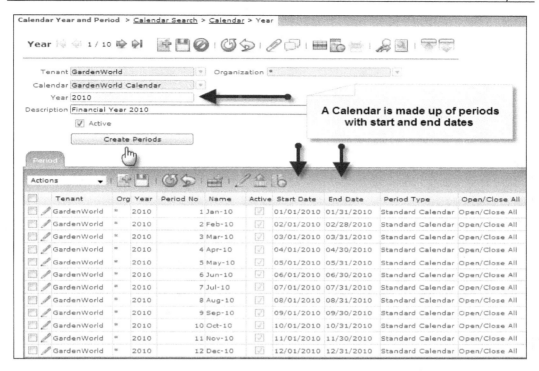

Once a year has been defined the **Create Periods** process will create the standard calendar periods from January to December. The screenshot above shows the 2010 year after the periods have been created. The user has to re-state calendar periods to the financial year and not be calendar-based.

Further to this is the important aspect of Period Document Control. Based on the system-defined document base types, a period can be opened or closed to allow or prevent a particular document type to be posted to that period. A typical example would be that Accounts Receivable (AR) invoices be closed for a past period but that General Ledger Journals (GL Journals) be allowed. It is critical within the enterprise that these rules are defined, and that monthly accounts department rules are set up to open and close these applicable periods.

Select a **Period** to see its control documents:

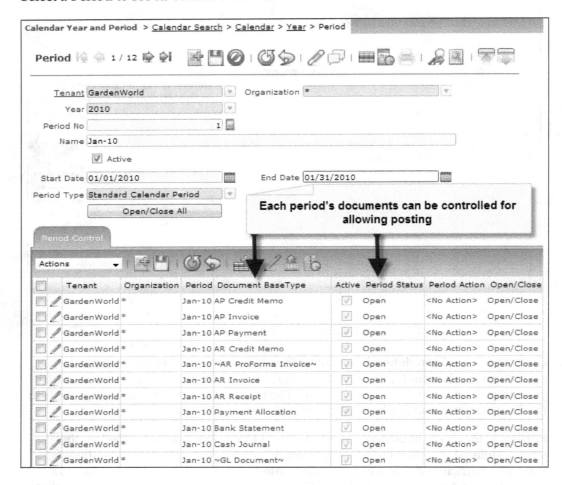

As from version 3 of Compiere, you can define different periods per organization.

# Account elements

As described in Chapter 2, Account elements are set up through the **Account Elements** menu item. In addition to defining the account, it's important to note that the tree level set-up of account elements define the core financial reporting structure:

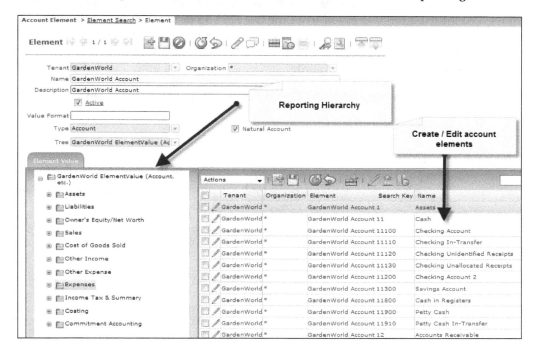

In the above example, the expenses reporting hierarchy is made up as follows:

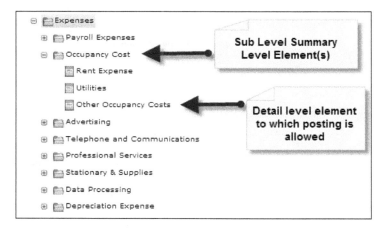

# Accounting schema and information dimensions

As described in Chapter 2, the Accounting Schema determines the information dimensions (referred to as Accounting Schema Elements) of the Compiere accounting entries. The information is derived from the transaction document. For instance, if a Compiere Activity has a mandatory field, the posting will fail if this field is not populated, or if it has an optional field, it will be used in the accounting entry if populated in the transaction document.

In the screenshot below, we add additional Accounting Schema Element to the Accounting Schema:

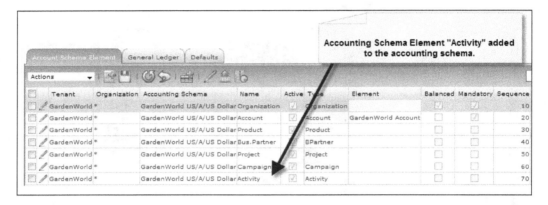

The system will now allow documents to be captured and post to this information dimension in the accounting entry posting:

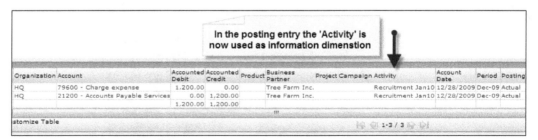

This additional information dimensional flexibility adds tremendous power to the reporting analysis within the enterprise.

# General Ledger (GL) document types

GL document base types determine the accounting entry principle to be used when posting the document. An Accounts Receivable (AR) accounting entry will be different from a physical inventory adjustment. The set-up is therefore that a Document Type (AR Invoice) is linked to an AR Invoice GL document type. This will thus determine the required accounting principles to be used per document transaction.

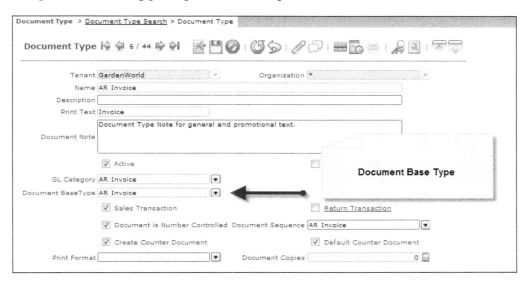

In the above example, the AR invoice document type and document base type are equivalent, but it is the base type that determines the actual accounting posting entry rule.

# Rules in processing accounting documents

There are certain rules within Compiere that must be adhered to in order for accounting entries to be processed:

- The timing of account postings (batch processing mode) are managed through a schedule set-up, and linked to the **Accounting Processor** window. You may bypass batch posting by the accounting processor by setting up the tenant to post documents immediately. This is done through the **Tenant** window.

- Transactions for accounting must be balanced. Where this fails, the balance is posted to a suspense balancing account set up through the accounting schema. If the suspense balancing is not allowed, the posting will be rejected with an error.

- Account elements must be active. If an account is not active, the booking is posted to a suspense account or is rejected, depending on the set-up.

- The currency conversion rate for the accounted currency (accounting schema) must be set up. If this fails, then the accounting entry will not be posted and is rejected by the system.

- The accounting periods must be open for the document type. If this fails, the document accounting is rejected, but can be re-submitted for posting. It is therefore critical that unposted documents be followed up on a regular basis. This is done through the **Unposted Documents** menu item.

- In a multi-organization implementation, the **Accounting Schema > General Ledger's** Due To and Due From accounts in the accounting schema are used to ensure accounting balance between organizations.

To view the accounting entry of a document, click on the **Posted** button on the document header, as follows:

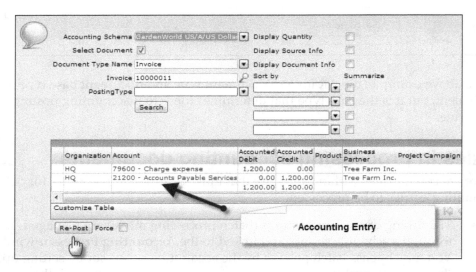

A very handy feature in Compiere is the ability to re-post a document. This can be used where the underlying document values or account structures have changed and re-posting is necessary.

# Accounting info view

The accounting info view is a handy view on the detail entries that make up an account balance.

To view the accounting info view, go to the **View>Account Info** menu item:

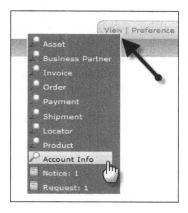

Enter your selection criteria, in order to view the accounting entries:

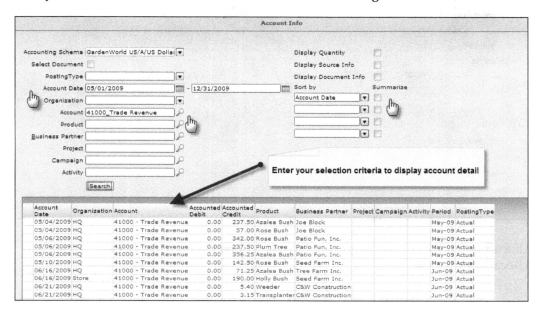

# Open item management

Compiere is, by default, an open item management system. This means that customer invoices and receipts (Sales Cycle) and purchasing invoices and payments (Payment Cycle) need to be allocated in order for the open balance on a document to be correctly reflected. Account statements are thus shown for the document on an open amount basis and not on a balance brought forward basis. Thus, in terms of accuracy of open amounts on documents, this requires discipline in the accounts department and also from customers and vendor reconciliations in order to reflect the correct statement of account at any given time. If this is not practical then an automated oldest invoice allocation process can be followed, but unless this is normal business practice in your industry or region, it is suggested that it is legally agreed with your customer.

Capturing a receipt from a customer or payment to a vendor is done through the **Payment** window:

Allocating receipts or payments to invoices is done through the **Payment Allocation** window:

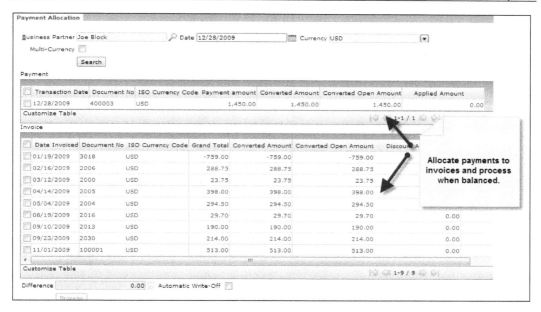

Allocating payments (customer receipts or vendor payments) to vendors creates an explicit allocation document. You can view this document in the **View Allocation** menu item, or link through from the payment or invoice window's **Allocations** tab.

# Payment selection—Paying vendors

Payment selection is the process of preparing the final payment remittances to suppliers. When the user selects the invoices to be paid, the system automatically:

- Allocates the payments to supplier invoices
- Prepares a remittance report showing which invoices are being paid
- Prepares an electronic file for bank upload (will need customization depending on bank requirements)
- Prepares a sequential check print where checks are used for payment

In Chapter 5 we saw a detailed review of the Payment to vendor process. The payment selection for individual vendor invoices is done through the **Payment Selection (manual)** menu item illustrated here:

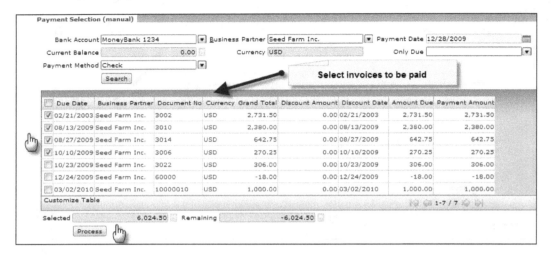

# Accounts Receivable and Payable Ledger Reconciliation

Because Compiere is document driven, the Accounts Receivable and Accounts Payable sub-ledgers are reconciled through the underlying document reports that make up those balances. In the open item environment, the open items balance to Accounts Receivable, and unallocated receipts and payments are separately reflected on the ledger. Prior to commencing any reconciliation process, make sure that you check all of the unposted documents, because an unposted document appearing on the report would not have an underlying accounting entry. This is done through the **Unposted Documents** menu item.

Accounts Receivable Ledger Account (This is the balance of open items receivable per customer documents):

1.  Set up an **Open Item** report showing open item amounts (either group by business partner or by invoice listing).
2.  Select the **Is Sales Transaction** checkbox when running the report. Select the **maximum** and **minimum** periods that reflect all documents.
3.  The total of this report must balance to the **Accounts Receivable** ledger.

Accounts Payable Ledger Account (This is the balance of open items payable per vendor document):

1. Set up an **Open Item** report showing open item amounts (either per business partner or per invoice).

2. Do not select the **Is Sales Transaction** checkbox when running the report. Select the **maximum** and **minimum** periods that reflect all documents.

3. The total of this report must balance to the **Accounts Payable** ledger account.

Unallocated receipts or payments (these are the receipts or payments not yet allocated to invoices):

1. Set up an unallocated payments report to split **Unallocated Receipts** and **Payments** (in the report select group **by Document Type**).

2. Make sure that you show the open payment amount total on the report.

3. Unallocated receipts will balance to the **Unallocated Receipts Ledger Account,** and unallocated payments will balance to the **Payment Selection Ledger account.**

> In a multi-currency environment, make sure that you set up different ledger accounts for Accounts Receivable, Payable, and the unallocated receipts and payment selection accounts *per* currency. Balance these accounts by selecting a different currency each time for the above reports.

# Cash management and banking reconciliation

To ensure that the bank general ledger account reflects the actual bank balance, Compiere specifies a specific document (**bank statement**) for each bank account. Bank reconciliation is the process of matching the actual bank statement to the system customer receipts and vendor payment entries. This must not be confused with allocations, which has a different purpose as described above.

There are two methods of capturing the actual bank statement:

1. Import the bank statement through the system import loader (recommended).

2. Recreate the bank statement for entries within the system (create lines from, or manual capturing of, bank statement lines).

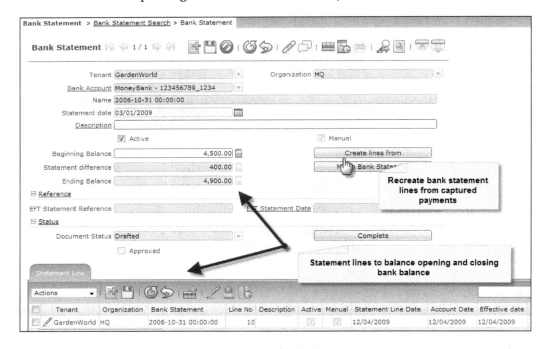

A bank statement line matched to a payment is as follows:

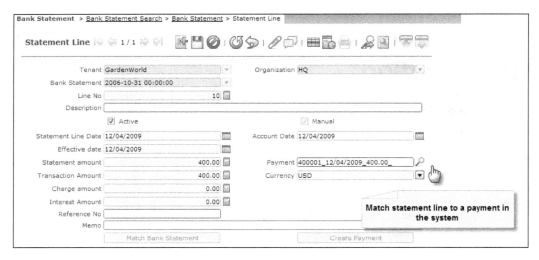

**Cash Journals** are similar to bank statements except that they reflect daily cash entries. These can be used for integrated daily point of sale takings, or for manual petty cash entries:

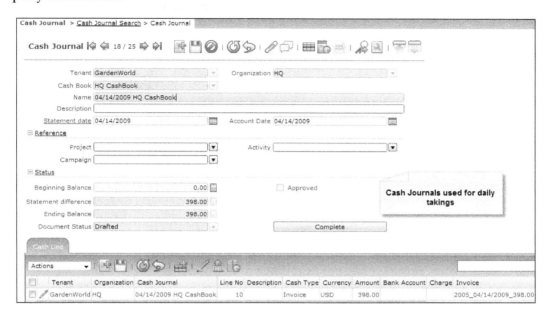

In order to **deposit** the daily takings into the bank a **cash journal** line needs to be captured, indicating the transfer from the cash ledger to the bank ledger:

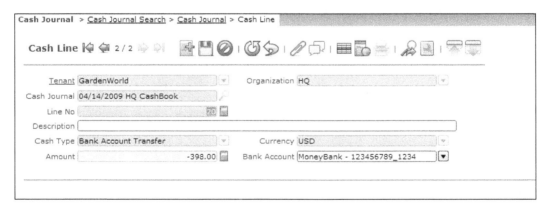

# The Bank in transit account reconciliation

The bank in transit account is the intermediatory control account for transactions between the actual bank account entries and the system entries. In short, this is the traditional bank reconciliation balance. Balances that are unreconciled are therefore items processed by the bank that are not in the system, or items in the system that have not been processed by the bank yet.

Run the **Unreconciled Payment** reports to reflect a list of such items:

| Compiere | | UnReconciled Payments | | Page 1 of 1 |
|---|---|---|---|---|
| **Parameter:** *Bank Account = MoneyBank - 123456789_1234* | | | | |
| Bank Account | Business Partner | Document No | Tender type | Payment Amt |
| MoneyBank - 123456789 - 1234 | Seed Farm Inc. | 400001 | Check | 400.00 |
| MoneyBank - 123456789 - 1234 | Seed Farm Inc. | 400002 | Check | 12.94 |
| MoneyBank - 123456789 - 1234 | Joe Block | 400003 | Check | 1,450.00 |
| Σ | | | | 1,862.94 |

The bank in transit account links intricately with the unreconciled payment or receipt items, as the accounting entries are as follows:

**Bank statement** *accounting (AR Receipts):*

| | Debit | Credit |
|---|---|---|
| Bank ledger account | DR (Receipts) | |
| Bank in Transit Account | | CR (Receipt in transit) |

**Payment** *accounting (AR Receipts):*

| | Debit | Credit |
|---|---|---|
| Bank in Transit Account | DR (Receipts not yet reconciled) | |
| Unallocated Receipts | | CR (Receipt not yet allocated to invoices) |

**Bank statement** *accounting (AP Payments):*

| | Debit | Credit |
|---|---|---|
| Bank in Transit Account | DR (Payments in transit) | |
| Bank ledger account | | CR (Payment) |

**Payment** *accounting (AP Payments):*

|  | Debit | Credit |
|---|---|---|
| Payment selection | DR (Payments not yet allocated to invoices) | |
| Bank in transit account | | CR (Payments not yet reconciled) |

As can be seen from the above tables, care must be taken to ensure that bank statements are reconciled (matched) on a regular basis to the system entries, and that receipts and payments are allocated to the respective invoices.

# Posting General Ledger journals (GL journals)

Because Compiere is document driven, the posting of manual GL journals is recommended only where no other document process is available. Posting to the main ledger accounts, such as Accounts Receivable, Accounts Payable, and Inventory Assets, is not recommended, as reporting on such accounts will be out of sync with the underlying documents making up those balances. GL journals are recommended as part of the financial year end process or raising accruals or specific non-system document-driven transactions, such as salaries, interest, allocations, corrections, and depreciation.

GL journals are posted in batch or individually. Posting GL journals in batch is done through the **GL Journal Batch** window:

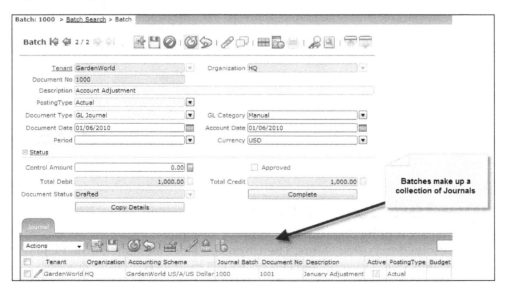

**Journals** make up batches that can be entered for different dates or currencies, depending on what is needed:

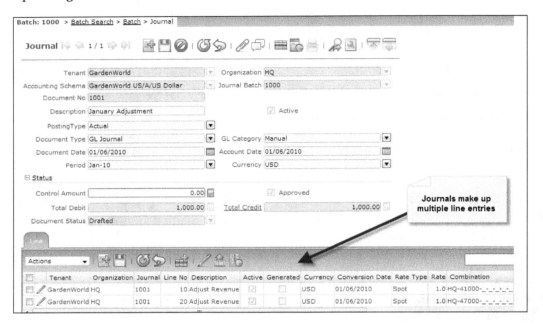

Adjusting the information layer reporting through Account **Combinations** on the entry lines is as follows:

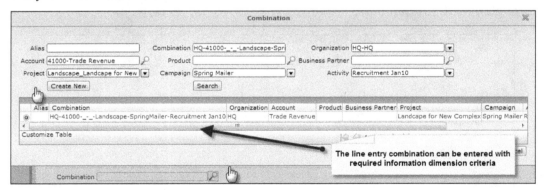

# Unposted documents

As part of the accounting department's monthly discipline, unposted documents should be resolved to posted status. The **Unposted Documents** window view will show documents that have not yet been processed by the accounting engine:

1. Zoom on these documents to view the source document and perform a further document action (complete/void), or to see why the document was not posted automatically.

2. Repost the document and ensure that the posting status has changed to **Posted**.

3. When finalized, the **Calendar Periods** may be closed to ensure that no documents are posted into closed or inactive periods.

To access the view of these documents, go to the **Unposted Documents** menu item:

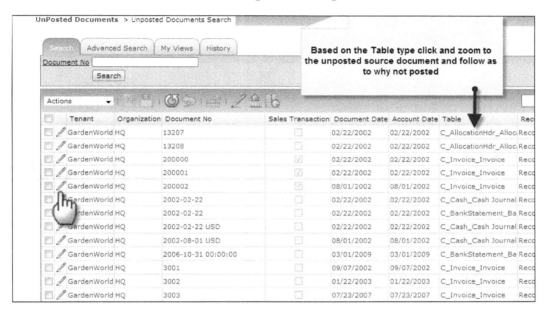

Click on the **Record Zoom** button to view the corresponding record that has not yet been posted:

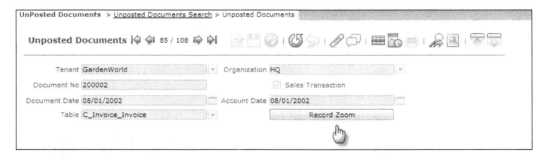

Where commitment accounting is not implemented, documents related to the C_Order table may be ignored. This includes Quotes, Sales Orders, and Purchase Orders, to name a few.

# Financial reporting

Financial reporting creates the management or control reports for the business. These include Profit/Loss Statements, Balance Sheets, CashFlow statements, or just custom monthly reports that are required.

A Financial Report is made up of the following columns and row sets:

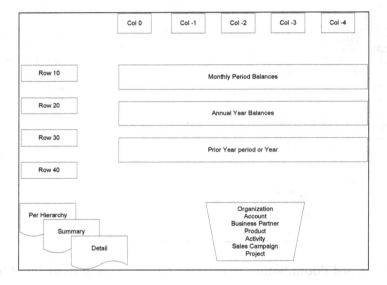

In the **Report Column Set**, a report column can be defined as:

- Period balance: A balance for the calendar period
- Year balance: A balance for the calendar year to date
- Debit balance: The total of the debit balances
- Credit balance: The total of the credit balances
- Calculation: A calculation (addition or, subtraction of columns)
- Relative to report selection period (0 = indicating current period, [-1 ], [-2 ], [-3], etc. indicating a period before selected period, and [+1] [+2] [+3] etc. indicating a period after selected period)

A Row Set is usually more complex than a Column Set and determines the lines and the source of the report. A line can be:

- **A line segment type that refers to the Accounting Schema elements** (meaning the Account or, in more complex circumstances, the information dimension such as Organization, Business Partner, Product, Campaign, etc )

- **Calculation** related to report variables

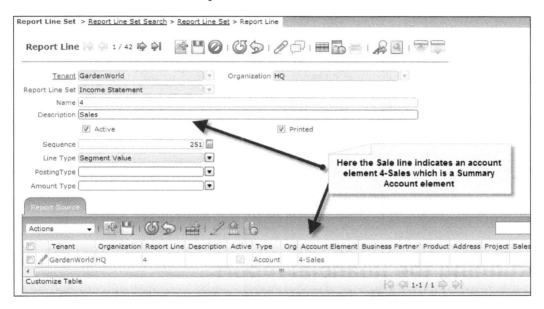

# Financial reporting hierarchy

The reporting hierarchy in Compiere is determined in the following manner:

**Organizational hierarchy:** In a multi-organizational structure, the reporting entity can be at either the summary or detail level, and the relationship is through parent-child trees. Thus, in Financial Reporting, a report either can be at the detailed organization level or can be rolled up into the summary level:

**Account element hierarchy:** In the same way as can be done for an organization tree, the account elements roll up into summary levels. Therefore, care must be taken to set up the accounting elements hierarchy for ease of use:

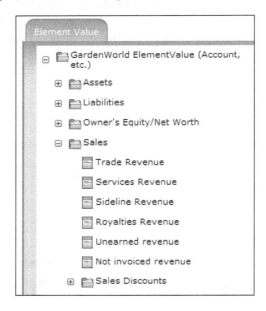

# Running the financial report

In running financial reports, the following process must be followed:

1.  Make sure to run the process to **Update Accounting Balances**. This will update the reporting tables from the latest accounting entries:

2. The **Financial Report** is run through the **Financial Report** menu item:

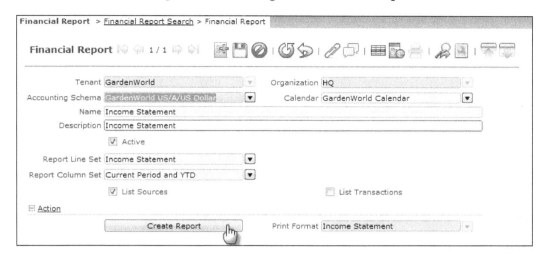

3. Define the report criteria for the financial report:

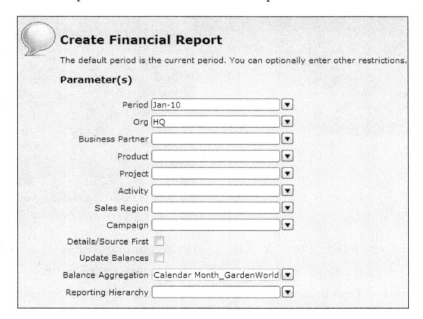

4. Review the report:

| | | Current Period | YTD |
|---|---|---|---|

Compiere        Income Statement        Page 1 of 2

**Parameter:**

| | | |
|---|---|---|
| Period | = | Jan-10 |
| Org | = | HQ |
| Details/Source First | = | N |
| Update Balances | = | N |
| Balance Aggregation | = | Calendar Month_GardenWorld US/A/US Dollar |

| Name | Description | Current Period | YTD |
|---|---|---|---|
| 4 | Sales | 0.00 | 0.00 |
| 49 | Sales Discounts | | |
| 4_ | Total Sales | 0.00 | 0.00 |
| 5 | Cost of Goods Sold | | |
| 55 | Returns | | |

# Other available financial reports

Compiere includes additional reports that can be used as a starting point for enterprise specific requirements:

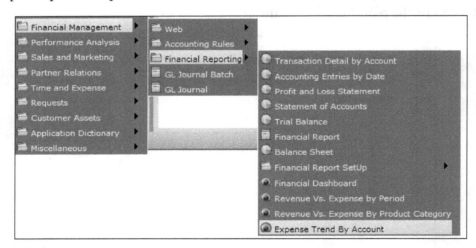

- **Transaction Detail by Account:** A list of accounting entries by account
- **Accounting entries by date**: Selected accounting entries by date
- **Profit and Loss Statement:** A quick report on the financial performance.
- **Trial Balance**: A trial balance listing
- **Balance Sheet**: A balance sheet on the position of the enterprise
- **Dashboards**: Financial dashboard (Revenue versus Expenses), by period and by Product Category.

- An example of the default **Balance Sheet** Business View report is as follows:

# Balance Sheet

### As Of 12/28/2009

| Asset | | |
|---|---|---|
| 12115 | Accounts Receivable Services - Trade | 9,649.90 |
| 12800 | Intercompany Due From | 2,060.07 |
| 14120 | Product asset | 32,819.60 |
| | Total Assets | 44,529.57 |
| Liability | | |
| 21100 | Accounts Payable Trade | 10,192.90 |
| 21101 | Tree Farm Payable | 11,266.70 |
| 21190 | Not invoiced receipts | 27,245.29 |
| 21800 | Intercompany Due To | 2,060.07 |
| | Total Liabilities | 50,764.96 |
| | Current Earnings | -6,235.39 |
| | Total Equity | -6,235.39 |
| | Total Liabilities & Equity | 44,529.57 |

- An example of the default **Profit and Loss Statement** Business View report is as follows:

# Profit & Loss Statement

### 01/01/2009 - 12/31/2009

| Income | | |
|---|---|---|
| 41000 | Trade Revenue | 9,136.90 |
| | Total Income | 9,136.90 |
| Expense | | |
| 51100 | Product COGS | 6,434.21 |
| 51210 | Product Cost Adjustment | 48.00 |
| 51290 | Product Inventory Clearing | 12,018.35 |
| 58100 | Invoice price variance | -3,785.17 |
| 58200 | Purchase price variance | -1,870.30 |
| 58300 | Purchase price variance Offset | 1,870.30 |
| 79600 | Charge expense | 111.00 |
| | Total Expense | 14,826.39 |
| | Net Income | -5,689.49 |

To edit the layouts of the above business view reports you need to go to the **External Report** menu item, in the **System Administrator** role. Here you will find the business view report's defined and the report source is loaded in the attachment to the report line, from where it can be edited:

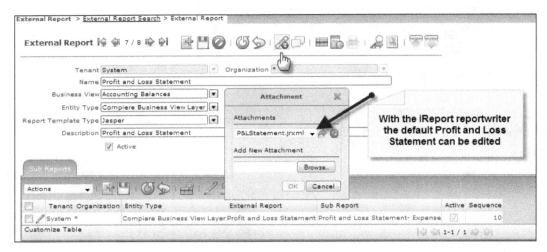

Shown below is the example of the Financial Dashboard:

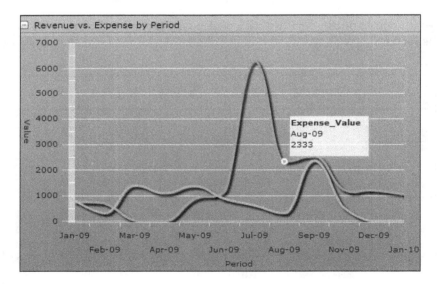

Business view reports and Dashboards are Compiere Professional and Enterprise edition features.

# Summary

With a separated accounting engine, through the JBoss application server, Compiere offers multiple layers of information, scalability, and capacity for business process customization, while still keeping within the normal rules of an accounting framework. What must be remembered is that the basic accounting rules per document type apply, and operationally it requires the normal disciplines in managing the accuracy and validity of the accounting entries.

We have touched on various system aspects of financial management. In this chapter we:

- Learnt an understanding of the Compiere accounting terminology
- Explained how accounting entries are derived from documents
- Showed you the accounting setups required in the system
- Explained open item management and the reconciliation of Accounts Receivable and Accounts Payable ledgers
- Explained the cash and bank management reconciliations
- Showed you how to find and follow up on unposted documents
- Overview of the Financial Reporting capabilities

Make sure to revisit the particular accounting entries, and the context per business cycle, that we covered in detail in previous chapters.

In the next chapter we will illustrate some avanced concepts in the system.

# 7
# Advanced Aspects

In the preceding chapters we illustrated the transactional processes of Compiere, and in this chapter we will be dealing with more advanced aspects of Compiere, including the following areas:

- Overview of the Compiere Application Dictionary and its components
- Adding a custom field in Compiere
- Setting up a basic document process approval workflow in Compiere

## The Compiere Application Dictionary (AD)

The Application Dictionary is what makes Compiere a truly unique and flexible business framework. Compiere was originally designed from the ground up on a **model driven architecture (MDA),** as defined by the **Object Management Group** (**OMG** — refer to www.omg.org). This means that the system design conforms to an open standard in its layered architecture between business, application, and platform logic. What MDA tries to achieve is to separate the business logic modeling, from technology modeling so as to ensure that both can evolve within their own domains, but still keeping within a framework of an open standard (and platform independent) that interconnects the two.

The benefit in the Compiere environment is that through modeling, design, and build the actual deployment time is greatly reduced. The AD also ensures a seamless upgrade of the platform while having little impact on the environment-specific business objects and processes.

The Application Dictionary of Compiere is meta data driven, meaning that contextual data defines the experience. This also means that the end user presentation layer and thus the **Graphical User Interface (GUI)** platform have been defined in different technologies (i.e. Java Swing, HTML, and Ajax) and offers endless possibilities.

The Application Dictionaries can be illustrated as follows:

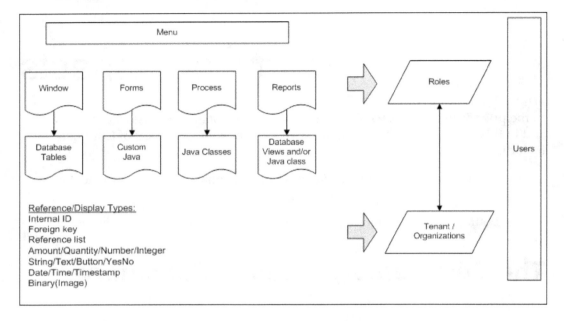

To access the Application Dictionary you need to log in as a System Administrator and refer to the following sub menu:

 We will use the Java Swing (Compiere Standard Edition) user interface for illustration purposes in this section.

The Application Dictionary consists of the following configuration.

# Table and columns

This refers to the fundamental building blocks of the system, and links Compiere data to the underlying Table and Column structures in the database. Illustrated below is the **Period** table in the AD that links to the underlying table name of **C_Period,** which you will find in the database:

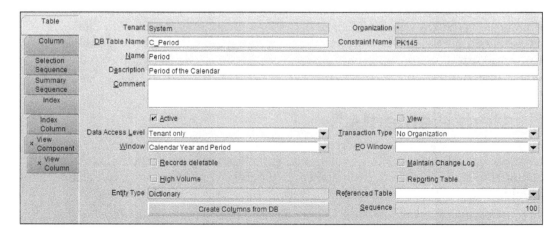

If the underlying database already contains the required fields, then by pressing the **Create Columns from DB** button and having the correct **DB Table Name**, Compiere will create the columns from the database in the AD.

Within a table, a key column must be created for use as the table identifier:

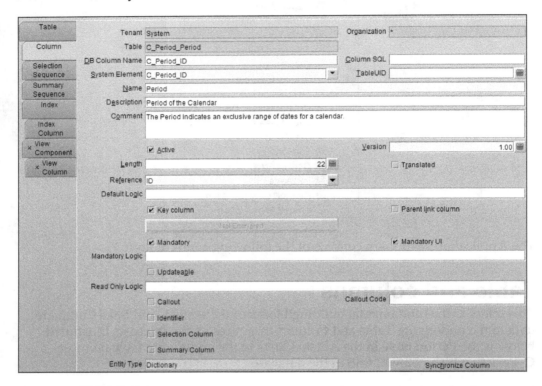

Illustrated is the key column **C_Period_ID**. A column links to a System Element, as explained below, and is linked to the underlying table through the **Synchronize Column** button. In effect, synchronization creates or updates a column to the underlying database.

# System elements

System elements are the common data elements and are used for central terminology references. These system elements link the underlying database columns to business-speak, for instance, in the following screenshot, **C_Period_ID** would be translated into the actual period:

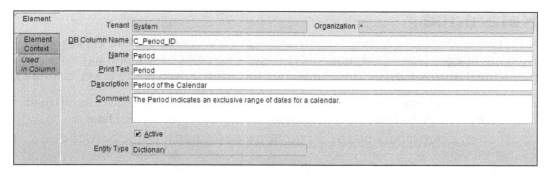

System elements are also used for setting up translations, as well as help comments on column fields.

# Validation rules

Field validation rules that are defined in the context of a column field are dynamically verified based on the predefined rules or user context, at time of rendering the data.

For instance when a Business Partner field is displayed for selecting, the Business Partner account must be active and not be a Summary Account as follows:

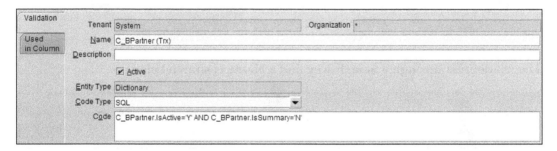

Based on the example shown above, a dynamic validation will be set up for the **C_BPartner_ID** column field (the Business Partner table key identifier) on the Order table, as follows:

# Reference

A Reference refers to database column field types that are either Data Types (i.e. an Amount, Integer, Date, Time, image, hyperlink, etc.) or a List validation (i.e. user pre-defined dropdowns) or Table validation (i.e. drop-downs for table key columns).

An example of a Data Type column would be a period start date. The Column field **StartDate** in the Period table in the database is defined as reference **Date**:

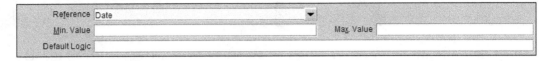

An example of a list validation on a **Period Control Action** (the actions that you can perform on a period) set-up is as follows:

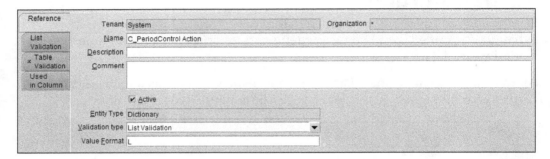

The list defined through a **Search Key** and a **Name** is shown below:

| Reference | | Tenant | Organization | Reference | Search Key | Name | Description |
|---|---|---|---|---|---|---|---|
| | 1 | System | * | C_PeriodControl Action | C | Close Period | Soft close - can be re-opened |
| List | 2 | System | * | C_PeriodControl Action | N | <No Action> | |
| Validation | 3 | System | * | C_PeriodControl Action | O | Open Period | |
| Table | 4 | System | * | C_PeriodControl Action | P | Permanently Close Period | |

Search keys are saved in the database.

Table Validations are data-defined based on existing referenced key columns and SQL selection. An example of a table reference would be a Document type based on a table validation SQL query. Herewith a Document type (**C_DocType**) is defined, but it refers to the appropriate Tenant/client so as to ensure that only the document types for a Tenant are displayed:

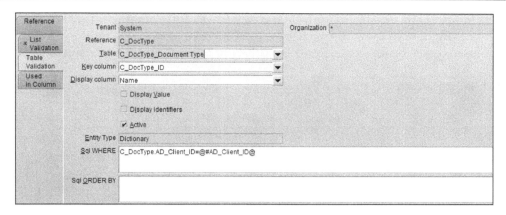

# Windows, Tabs, and Fields

Compiere generates all of its windows in a standard dynamic way by reference to the defined AD. This AD window thus relates to setting up the Windows, and the Tabs (sub-linked windows) and Fields that are displayed on those Windows.

Illustrated here is an example of the Calendar and Period window that defines the structure of the periods within Compiere:

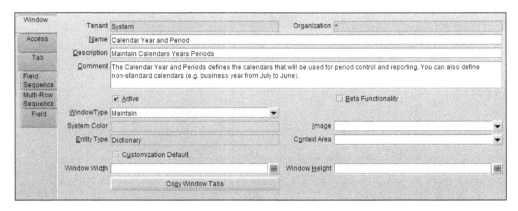

Windows may be of the following **Window Types**:

- **Maintain:** Usually used in the context of master data, such as Business Partner or Products.

- **Query Only:** A window type that is used for displaying results in a grid, and is not editable.

- **Transaction**: A window type used for transaction processing , such as an order or an invoice.

The Window **Tabs** refer to the sub-linked windows of the main window header, or the preceding tab. In the example below, the Calendar window is built by defining the Calendar, applicable Year, Period and Period control, and Non Business Day:

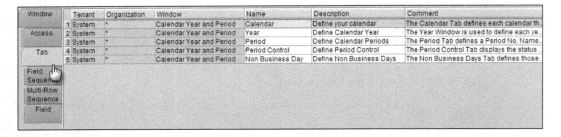

The window's **Fields** are populated from the Table and Columns associated with the window:

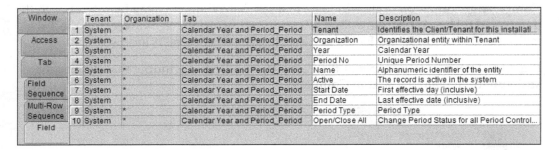

# Forms

Forms are windows that are not automatically generated through the AD but are static and are usually for custom purposes, based on specific Java code classes.

Below is a Form that defines the File Import Loader process:

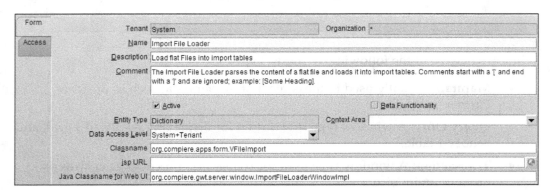

Once a Form has been defined, it is linked to the Java classes through the **Classname** (Swing) and **Java Classname for Web UI fields**. These classes will contain the source code to build these custom Forms.

# Info windows

These are windows that are used for quick searches and information views.

Here is the **Info window** for viewing invoices. It is defined through an SQL query on a table and then defining the columns within the Info Window:

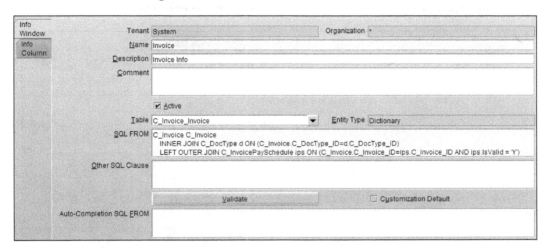

# Report Views

Where database views may exist within the underlying database, the AD requires the Database views to be defined in the system in order to be accessible.

Here is an example of the **Invoice** database view for a week:

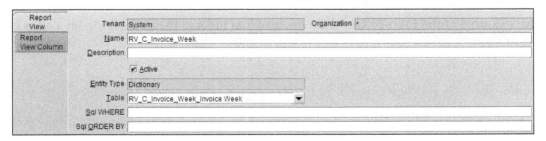

To distinguish them from normal tables, Compiere uses the **RV_** prefix convention to name a Report View within the underlying database.

# Reports and processes

These are used to set up reports (link to a Report view) or a process that can link to a Java code class. Reports and processes may have parameters that define a selection process. Examples of a report would be an invoice enquiry, and an example of a process would be to generate invoices from orders.

Here is the actual **Report** that defines the **Invoices per week** report:

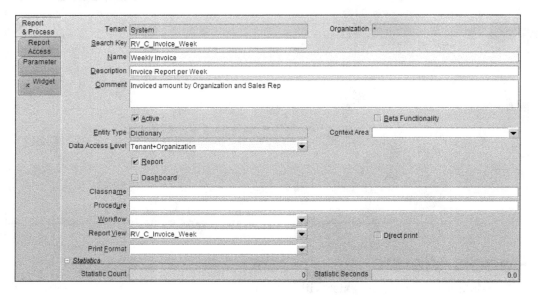

Reports may have access restrictions and selection parameters. If a report is also displayed as a Dashboard (Compiere Enterprise version 3.5 onwards) then an underlying dashboard widget needs to be defined.

An example of the **Invoice Generate Process** that links to the underlying Java class is as follows:

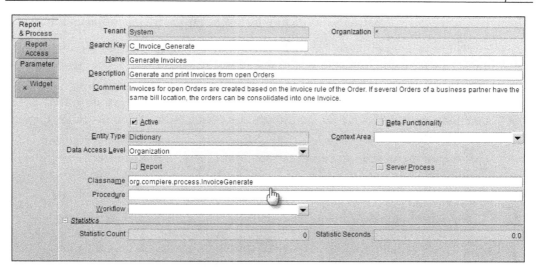

In windows, Buttons may be linked to processes (i.e. **C_Invoice** Copy From which copies lines from other invoices on the Invoice windows) and Processes need not all be manually run as such. Processes can be defined as server processes, and can also be scheduled through the Compiere scheduler.

# Setting up a Compiere menu item

The user menu is your default tree, and is accessed through the System Administrator role. You can find the **Menu** item in the screen tree:

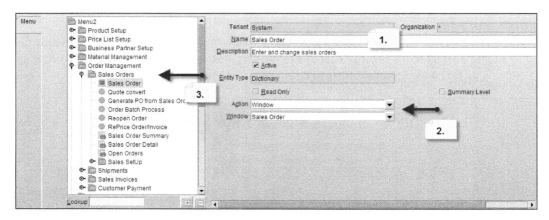

The above screenshot illustrates a typical window set-up, which is done as follows:

1. Create a new menu item by clicking on the **New** button. Enter a name and a description.

2. Define its action type: A menu item's action type can be a Window, Form, Process, Report, Task, or Workflow. Link an AD item to the menu, which is illustrated above, where window **Sales Order** is linked to the **Sales Order** menu item.

3. Move the menu item in context of the main menu tree for users understanding and access.

>
> It is recommended that you define your own windows, or copy from the existing dictionary, for customizations. Because dictionary (system) defined items may be overwritten during the process of migrating to a new version, it is better to copy a window and customize it in the copied window (or create new). This applies to Java code as well: never change the original source as it may be overwritten during migration.

# Adding a new field to a window and database

In this section we are going to illustrate how the System Administrator would go about adding a new field to the database. As an illustration, we are going to add a probability reference field that can be used to measure a predefined set of outcomes on an order to the **Sales Order** window.

1. Find the context by Zooming to the Table from the Window. Open and find the **Sales Order** window in the **Window, Tab, and Field** menu item when logged in as System Administrator:

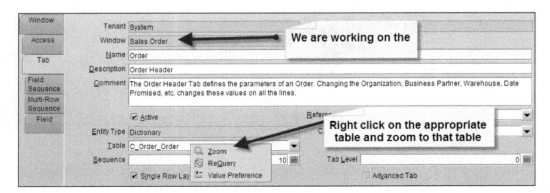

2.  Zoom from the window into the underlying **Table and Column** window. Order records are maintained in the database in the **C_Order** table:

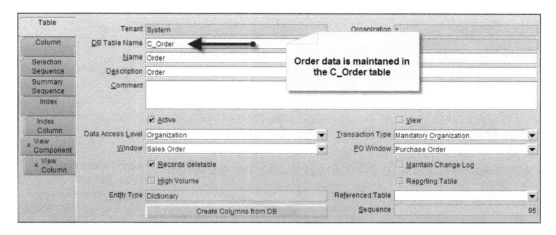

3.  Next we refer the **Column** tab, and create a new column in the table (see the field naming conventions below). The new column must be as a **System Element** defined and hence we need to create a **System Element** prior to using it as a **Column** in the Table:

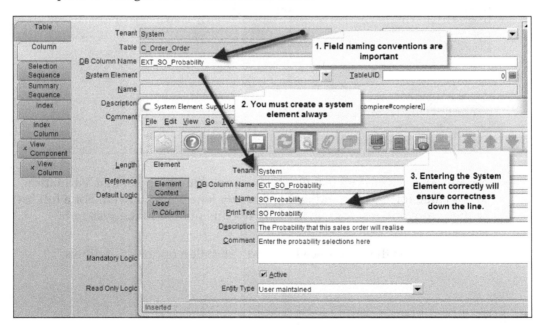

4. Once the **System Element** has been defined, we set up the **Column** as follows:

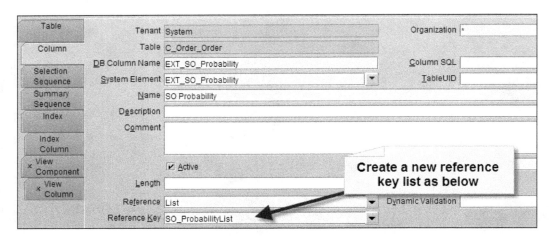

5. Create a new **Reference key** as follows:

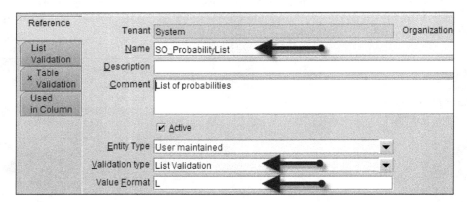

Because this is a custom list, we choose a validation type of **List Validation,** and a value format of **L,** indicating that any letters are allowed. For a full list of these conventions, refer to the help documentation in the system by pressing *F1*.

6. We then define the **Reference** key's list validation options as follows:

| Reference | | Tenant | Organization | Reference | Search Key | Name | Description | Active | Entity Type |
|---|---|---|---|---|---|---|---|---|---|
| | 1 | System | * | SO_ProbabilityList | U | Unknown | | ✔ | User maintained |
| List | 2 | System | * | SO_ProbabilityList | A | Average | | ✔ | User maintained |
| Validation | 3 | System | * | SO_ProbabilityList | V | Very Likely | | ✔ | User maintained |
| ✕ Table | 4 | System | * | SO_ProbabilityList | N | Not Likely | | ✔ | User maintained |
| Validation | 5 | System | * | SO_ProbabilityList | E | Excellent | | ✔ | User maintained |
| Used in Column | | | | | | | | | |

7. The finalized column (and thus the ultimate window field) set-up is thus shown as follows:

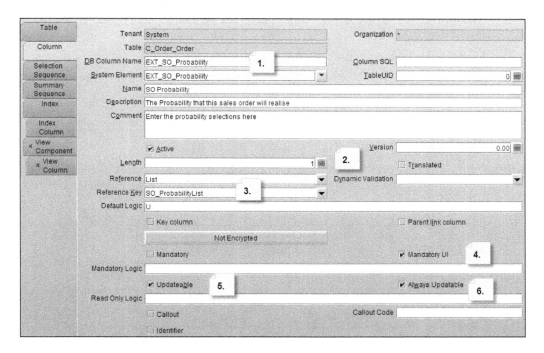

We finalize the set-up of the field by indicating:

1. **Field naming conventions**: Compiere recommends that customer-specific table and database column names be prefixed by **EXT_**, **XX_**, or **CUST_**, or the four letter entity registered with Compiere, such as **SAAC_**. This would also apply to indexes and constraints. The reason for this is that these entities are ignored in the migration process.

2. **Length of field**: Because we know that for this particular field there is going to be only one character we define a length of **1**.

3. **Default logic**: We assume **U**, based on our list being Unknown.

4. **Mandatory UI**: Indicates that this field will be mandatory in the window, but not at database level.

5. **Updatable**: Indicates that the field is editable.

6. **Always Updatable**: Indicates that the field is always updatable, regardless of document status.

## Final step in column creation—Create / Synchronize with the database

The final step in the process of creating a field is to make sure that it is synchronized to the underlying database from the AD. Scroll down on the column tab to find the **Synchronize Column** button, as shown in the example below:

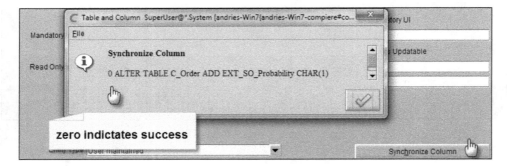

# Adding our custom field to the Order window

Back in the menu item Window, Tab, and Field (find the **Sales Order** window) > **Tab** (header/top level):

1. Click on the **Create Fields** button to add the field to the database:

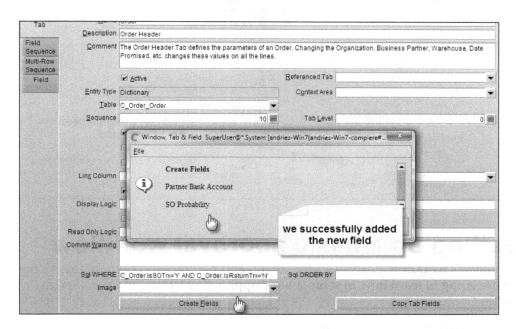

2. Change the desired sequence of the field to the correct position in the list of fields:

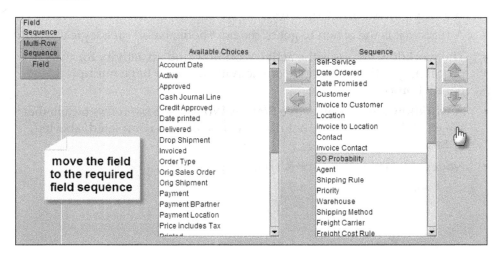

3. Re-open the appropriate **Sales Order** window to display the field:

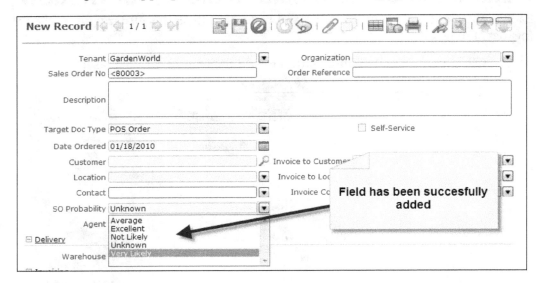

# Setting up a basic approval workflow

Compiere's workflow processes form an integral part of the system. In this section we are going to learn how to setup a basic approval workflow for a document within Compiere.

The system definitions are as follows:

- A workflow is made up of a *node* and *transitions*.
- A *node* refers to a piece of work.
- A *transition* is the action to get to the next node, based on a logical *condition*.
- The workflow *process* is the active workflow and an activity for the processing of the active node (an activity also may have multiple parallel processes).
- A workflow also has an active *State*. A Workflow *State* refers to whether the workflow is running, not running, not started, completed, aborted, or terminated.
- Nodes also have *Owners* or *Responsible* persons.

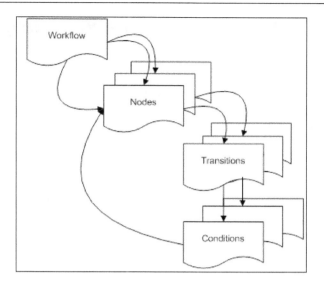

# Illustrative workflow example

We are going to set up a workflow between two roles, whereby the **Gardenworld** Purchasing role will capture a Purchase Order and the order will be approved by the **Gardenworld** User role. This type of approval requires a flag, and Compiere has a built in **IsApproved** database field that is used for this purpose.

> Compiere has standard document workflows and transitions that are predefined within its workflow processes. These nodes are **DocStart**, **DocPrepare**, **DocComplete**, and **DocAuto** (automatic approval). What this means is that workflow processes already manage the transitions of documents, with the System being the Owner of these workflow nodes.

# Defining a custom node in a workflow

We use the workflow editor to define a new node.

1. Open the Workflow editor window, and find the Order process **Process_Order**. Right-click in the editor, and then add an additional new node called **Order Approval**:

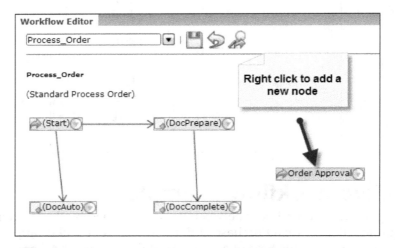

2. We need to define where the transition is going to take place by defining the originating node (**Document prepare**) and the next node (**Document complete**):

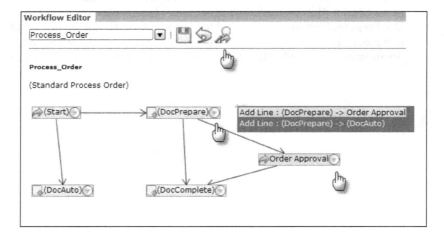

3. Click on the upper-right Zoom button to zoom to the actual workflow process, and find the newly-created node:

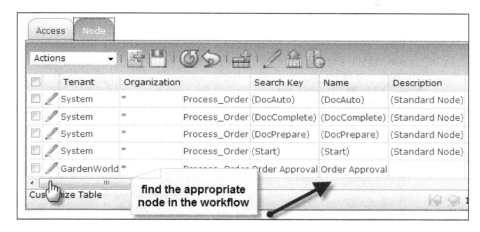

4. Define the node's owner by creating a workflow owner. Right-click on the **workflow owner** field:

5. The node's workflow owner is set to be role-based, as follows:

6.  The Node for Approval can be summarized as follows:

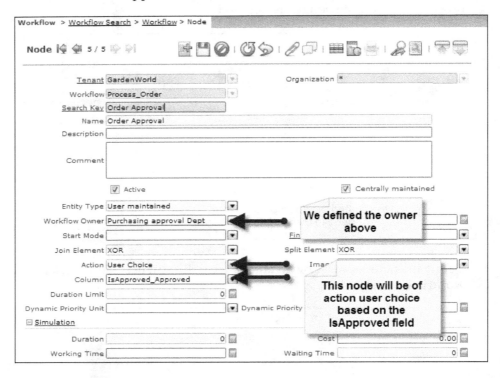

7.  Define the **Transition** of the node through a condition:

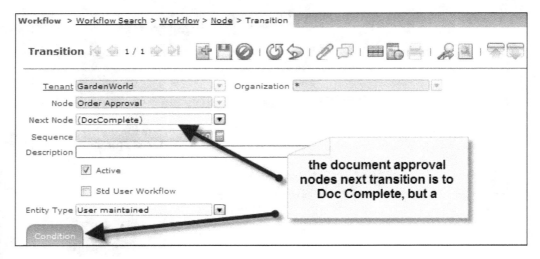

The **condition** we set up for the document workflow to transition to Document Complete is as follows:

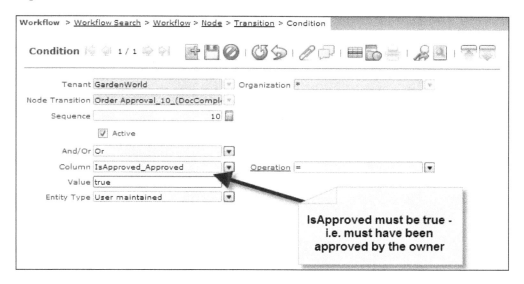

# Testing the workflow

We can now illustrate the workflow by creating an order and ensuring that it gets approved correctly.

1.  We log in as the **GardenWorld Purchasing** role, as follows:

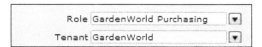

2.  Create a Purchase Order, and then click on the **Complete** button. The Order will be placed in an **In Progress** status, because the workflow's next node is document approval:

3. We log off, and then log back in to the system with the **GardenWorld User** role (workflow owner):

4. Find the **Workflow Activities** menu item, and then approve the document, as follows:

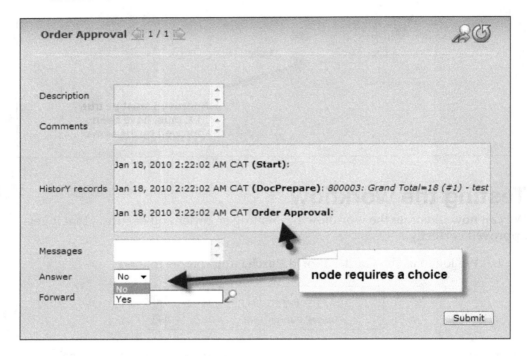

5. The Document will be approved when the owner sets the approval **status** to **Yes**:

# Summary

We have covered certain aspects with regards to Compiere in this chapter—namely the Application Dictionary (AD) and Workflows, as follows:

- We gave you an overview of the Compiere Application Dictionary components.
- We illustrated how to add a menu item and a custom list field to a Compiere window by using the AD components.
- We gave you an overview of the Compiere Workflow processes, and illustrated how this is set up.

In the next chapter we will illustrate some core concepts in the project implementation of Compiere.

## Summary

# Project Planning for Go-Live and Beyond

**8**

In this chapter, highlight some of the project planning aspects of getting to the Compiere system's go-live milestone and beyond. We will cover:

- The issues around the people involved in the project
- Overview of aspects regarding technical and functional environments
- The go-live milestone
- Identifying aspects regarding post-implementation, including support
- An overview of keeping Compiere up-to-date, and its migration process

## Managing people (and the project) for success

A **system** could be defined as an abstract entity that maintains its existence through the mutual interaction of its components/actors. The success of these interactions is determined by an organizations' people. From the outset of a new implementation project, it is required of management to engage, manage, motivate, and evaluate the people involved in the project, throughout the duration of the project.

# Finish with the people you start with

Implementing an ERP system requires significant change and buy-in throughout the business. People will learn new skills and work in a new or different way. This requires decision making, as well as a top-down approach within the company structures. In realising the changes required, it is thus important to note that the key people within the project be identified early, and that they be appropriately incentivized to stay on board for the duration of the project. These key staff members may include the original project initiators, key project members, and user staff members that know the aspects of the business very well. Also important will be the investment in such staff members from a training point of view. The key to success is to ensure that the new knowledge is contained within the project and within the organization for as long as possible.

On conclusion of the project, it is also important for these staff members to be available, because for a while they will be the key people that users and management refer to for the detailed knowledge and impact of business process and system requirements.

# The people you start with are not necessary the people you end-up with

An integrated ERP environment may not have every person in the organization's buy-in, and users and management that do not buy in to the processes need to be identified and appropriately addressed as soon as possible. The best outcome is that these users are specifically re-trained in their area, or that their concerns are addressed through the correct channels. But even with all of the change management, communication, project meetings, and functional training, some users still either see a new system as a threat or simply just don't buy in to the new processes, because they may be adverse to change. These types of users create a negative atmosphere and may, in extreme circumstances, cause deliberate damage to the process. Sadly, these users often sabotage the project before they even have the necessary information and experience to make an informed decision.

# Project communication and follow up

It is critical for the communication level within the project to be appropriate for the different stages of the project. The key driver in change management process is communication. Communication has many forms, and includes staff conferences, posters-on-the-wall, meetings, email, web portals, events, forums, surveys, or any format currently used within the organization to communicate issues.

The project will start to fail when action items are not communicated and followed through within the timeframe required. Action items should be communicated after every meeting, and accountability assigned. The status of such items should be followed up consistently and reported with the aim of ensuring consistent transparency and corrective action prior to getting serious issues that could affect the project further down the line. The key to communication is that it instils confidence throughout the project and the organization. Key issues and decisions should be communicated by management and not by the project, as communication by management will reinforce the perception that business is taking ownership of the processes.

No project can be a success without key management buy-in at the appropriate decision-maker level, and at the level of detail required. Whether that is at CEO, CFO, or CIO level depends on the issue, but it is important that they be the drivers of the process.

# Project documentation control

Another foundation for the success of the project is documentation control. This is true for any size of project, and entails the following:

- **Appropriate project templates and sign-off**: Regardless of the project methodology, document templates formalize the process and commit all parties to the agreed process, and sign-off ensures appropriate accountability.

- **Compiling and managing documentation for business process knowledge**: A tremendous amount of knowledge builds up during an ERP implementation, and it is important to document this.

- **Documentation of testing**: Testing processes and results should be documented and agreed upon.

- **Documentation of technical aspects**: The IT infrastructure team should ensure that all technical aspects of the project are appropriately documented.

- **End user training documentation**: It is critical that this be relevant and up-to-date with the latest changes, and should be simple enough for new users to easily understand.

- **Managing documentation repositories:** There is no point in having documentation if it cannot easily be accessed by the correct user. Whether this is done on an electronic Wiki basis, through the use of shared directory repositories, or through traditional lever arch files, it should be natural and should fit the business.

# Technical and infrastructure go-live

In most cases, considerations for new hardware or change in operational structure is advised with a new ERP system.

## Hardware and environment for development and testing

Having a test or sandbox environment is critical, as this facilitates experimental changes and also verifies particular system and process scenarios by the implementation and development team.

The environment for development and testing should be formalised, and very often time is wasted on re-installation and re-configuration of the test environment when appropriate controls would have avoided this. Such controls include:

- Ensuring a clear split between the development and formal test environment, to facilitate controlled feedback and release staging.
- Subversion control of source code and deployment files: Subversion is a software engineering tool for controlling different versions of source code for tracking, comparison, or roll back.
- A Backup strategy for development, test data, and the production environment, each of which will require a different strategy.
- A Fail over and server redundancy strategy entailing a cloned development and test environment, for easy recovery depending upon time requirement.

## Hardware and environment for production

The hardware and operational environment for the production system should meet the business requirements, and should consider any anticipated short-to-medium term future growth.

Key decisions regarding this environment include the following:

- Hosted versus on-premise installation
- Stress testing and performance tuning
- Network and security environment
- Back-up strategy for the production environment.

# Hosted versus on-premise installation

With the changing data centre environments, and due to Compiere being a web-based system, it is very often beneficial to host the server at a data centre versus on the customer's premises. The Compiere Cloud Edition also facilitates hosting within the Amazon EC2 cloud computing environment. There are also options available from Compiere partners to run Compiere as a service, or run it within private Virtual Machine (VM) clouds. Following are the new decisions affecting the ERP environment, the answers to which will depend on the critical factors important to the business:

- **Cost**: Often, hosted environments have a lower cost of ownership, because data centres provide better hardware scalability and redundancy environments, and the up-front investment costs of a new environment may not make sense. If the enterprise has existing infrastructure then the cost benefit of using a hosted environment may not be realised and an on premise solutions may be advisable.

- **Data integration issues**: With the advance of Webservices (SOA) standards, data integration decisions are pretty much the same, regardless of whether data is hosted or is on-premise. Legacy integration systems may dictate that localized access is required.

- **Control and security issues**: For many businesses' risk and legal profile, the business may prefer to remain in control of their systems on premise or hosted.

# Stress testing and performance tuning

Because of the tremendous growth in hardware advances, infrastructure risk is certainly much lower than it was 10 years ago. However, under sizing of the infrastructure is much harder to fix than before due to complexity. It is important to stress-test the transactional and operational aspects of the production environment prior to go-live. The overall architecture must meet the operational requirements of the system. Hardware issues pertaining to performance are RAM, CPU benchmarking, and data I/O and load balance monitoring. Performance tuning of the Oracle database and Tomcat/JBoss application server environment is critical in a particular environment, and would differ depending on transactional volumes and number of concurrent users as well as data storage requirements.

A large system architecture environment scenario could dictate multiple application servers and a single database server configured in clusters:

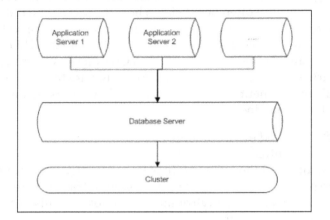

 Compiere can support multi-server environment license and product options depending on a particular environment.

# Network and security environment

While standard networks these days are pretty fast and reliable the main issues around the production environment are firewalls, browser security, client anti-virus software, and remote access policies. It is critical that these aspects be tested up front, and that appropriate firewall and security environment changes and policies be put in place.

# Backup-strategy

The operational back up strategy should back up the following:

- Operating system jobs and scripts.
- Compiere source code, SUN Java, and Subversion repositories.
- Compiere2 directory, which includes all of the deployment files.
- Data repositories. Usually these are backed up to the `Compiere2\data` directory, but may be set up differently, in order to accommodate the back-up strategy. Different real-time back-up strategies could also affect production performance.

# The go-live milestone

We will address the go-live in two aspects: namely, the technical go-live and the functional go-live.

## The technical go-Live

During the technical go-live, the following aspects should be in place:

- Synchronization of the development environment and the production environment should be finalized. A clear cut-off, in terms of functionality that is implemented and functionality that is not implemented (i.e. those that are left for a later phase or that are not critical for go-live) should be communicated to the management and users.

- All master data and operational data required for go-live should be finalized and be ready for upload.

- Hardware servers and software should now be in a redundant environment.

- The network environment and settings should be finalized and in place.

- Lock down access to the system to prevent changes being made accidentally.

- Technical sign-off by the infrastructure management.

## The functional go-live

The goal of a go-live is to ensure that it is as much of a non-event as possible. When the systems starts functioning for users it should be reflective of the processes as designed and agreed. User should have been through test scenarios and be capable of handling basic system functions:

- Super users and system trainers should be on hand to assist with the issues that arise, and there may be a list of repetitive questions that can be clearly communicated. Compile a daily list of these questions and communicate the answers to staff where relevant.

- A help desk should be ramped up where there are many users that can use a call centre environment.

- The project team should meet daily to address the most pertinent issues and give feedback to the management team and users.

- Regular management meetings with the project team should be in place so as to ensure feedback at the correct levels of the project.

# A Compiere standard implementation project plan

The following briefly depicts a standard Compiere implementation project plan, which will include:

- **The Pre-implementation phase:** This would include the sales, negotiation, and scoping of the requirements.

- **The Implementations phase:** This phase includes the setting up of infrastructure, development, and training aspects.

- **The Go Live:** This is the time of data migration from the old environment to the new, as well as users starting to use the new environment.

- **The post implementation phase:** This phase involves finalizing procedures documentation, snaglists, and maintenance.

- **Project closure:** This includes the aspects of agreement such as hand-over of ownership to the enterprise.

## The Compiere pre-implementation project plan

This phase of the project involves pre-sales, scoping, and defining user requirements and finalizing the negotiations regarding costing and other requirements. Aspects of the project plan can be illustrated as follows:

```
− Compiere Standard Implemenation Project
    − Pre-Implementation Phase
        − Pre-Sales Phase
            Understand the clients business
            Setup Demos and workshops
            Prospect Feedback
        − Scoping and User Requirements Phase
            Gather detail user requirements (As Is)
            Determine the To-Be processes
            Gap Analysis, SWOT, Best Practice Workshops
            Obtain list of current and required reports
            Finalise process flow documentation
            Final Process flow sign-off
        − Negotiation Phase
            Determine project pricing
            Negotiation
            Finalise Contract
    + Implementation Phase
    + Go Live
    + Post-Implementation Phase
    + Project Closure
```

# The implementation project plan

The aspects of the implementation phase will include the infrastructure environment, the initial assessment of data, development of customizations, configuring the system to user requirements, and is illustrated as follows over the next five illustrations:

- Project plan illustration 1: Implementation plan.

```
─ Compiere Standard Implemenation Project
  + Pre-Implementation Phase
  ─ Implementation Phase
    ─ Prepare Environment
      ─ Confirm Environment
          Verify Network & Servers
          Verify Software Installed
      ─ Initial Assessment
          Prepare Tenant Data
          Prepare accounting Chart of Accounts
          Prepare Customer, Vendor Data
          Prepare Inventory Product Data
          Prepare Product Pricing Data
          Output Documents Stationery Layouts : Orders, Invoices, Delivery Notes
        Determine Time needed to prepare Data
    ─ Customisation and enhancements
        Scoping and workshops
        Programming, Testing, Setup Release Cycle, etc
        Client Sign-off
    ─ Installation
        Install Compiere and Database
        Tenant Setup
        Setup Training Environment with sample data
    ─ Compiere Overview Training
        User Interface
        Query Windows, Reports
        Attachment
        Zoom Across
        Value Preferences
```

- Project Plan illustration 2: Implementation plan continues.

| |
|---|
| Report & Print |
| User Practice Workshop |
| − Basic Configuration |
|   − Tenant Configuration |
|     Tenant Setup |
|     Organization Setup |
|     Chart Of Accounts & Accounting Elements, Charges |
|     Financial Periods |
|     Tax Setup, Currency, UOM (Unit of Measure) |
|     Banks & Cash Books |
|     Products |
|     Payment Terms |
|     Users and Roles |
|     Menu Setup |
|     Alerts and Schedulers |
|     Workflows |
|     Operating System and Database Jobs and scripts |
|   − Business Partners |
|     Business Partner Master Data and Accounting |
|   − Material Management |
|     Product |
|     Product Attributes |
|     Pricing : Price Lists, Discount Schema |
| Do an Initial Data Import |
| − Business Process Flow implement |
|   − Sales Cycle |
|     Quotation : Binding and Non Binding |
|     Sales Order, Credit Order, Point of Sale Orders |
|     Customer Invoice |

- Project Plan illustration 3: Implementation plan continues.

| |
| --- |
| Customer Shipments |
| Commission |
| Customer Returns |
| Hands On Training : Sales Process |
| ⊟ **Purchasing Cycle** |
| Requisition |
| Purchase Order |
| Material Receipt |
| Vendor Invoice |
| Vendor Returns |
| Matching PO, Invoice, Material Receipt |
| Hands On Training: Purchase Cycle |
| ⊟ **Material Management** |
| Product, Product Categories, Product Accounting |
| Product Pricing |
| Inventory Movement |
| Physical Inventory |
| Internal Use Inventory |
| Replenishment |
| Inventory Reporting |
| ⊟ **Product Costing** |
| Costing Setup |
| Update Product Costs |
| ⊟ **Material Confirmations** |
| Material Receipt Confirmation |
| Shipment Confirmation |
| Movement Confirmation |
| ⊟ **Relationship Management** |
| Lead and Customer Management |
| Credit Management |

- Project Plan illustration 4: Implementation plan continues.

| |
|---|
| Partner Relations |
| Counter Documents |
| − **Project Management** |
| Project Order |
| Project Issue |
| − **Request Management** |
| Request Categories, Workflow |
| Request |
| Issue Tracking |
| − **Financials** |
| − **Accounts Receivable** |
| AR Receipt |
| Dunning Statements setup |
| Recurring Documents |
| Aging Reports |
| Open Item reports |
| − **Accounts Payable** |
| AP Payments |
| Payment Allocation |
| Payment Selection |
| AP Invoices and AP Credit notes |
| Open Item reports |
| Unallocated Payment Reports |
| − **Banking** |
| Bank Statement |
| Bank Reconciliation |
| Unreconciled Banking Reports |
| − **General Ledger** |
| Charges |
| GL Journals |
| Cash Journal |

- Project Plan illustration 5: Implementation plan continues.

| |
|---|
| Understand Underlying Accounting Engine |
| − Financial Reporting |
| Profit & Loss Reporting |
| Trial Balance |
| Tax Reporting |
| − Business Views & Dashboards |
| Setup Business Views, Jasper Reporting |
| Setup Dashboard views |
| − Live Data Import |
| Import Business Partners, Products |
| Enter or import Open AR & AP Invoices |
| Enter or import opening Trail Balances |
| + Go Live |
| + Post-Implementation Phase |
| + Project Closure |

# The go-live milestone project plan

The go-live milestone includes infrastructure and the functional go-live of the systems as follows:

| |
|---|
| − Compiere Standard Implemenation Project |
| + Pre-Implementation Phase |
| + Implementation Phase |
| − Go Live |
| − Technical Infrastructure Go-live |
| Production Servers |
| Backup and Failover Strategy |
| − Functional Go-Live: |
| End User Processes & Procedures |
| Month-End Processes & Procedures |
| + Post-Implementation Phase |
| + Project Closure |

# Post implementation

The post implementation phase of the implementation covers snaglists, finalizing documentation, maintenance, and user training, as follows:

| |
|---|
| ⊟ Compiere Standard Implemenation Project |
|    ⊞ Pre-Implementation Phase |
|    ⊞ Implementation Phase |
|    ⊞ Go Live |
|    ⊟ Post-Implementation Phase |
|       Resolve Outstanding Issues |
|       Refine Implementation Documentation |
|       Post Implementation Support and maintenance |
|       Post Implementation Enhancements |
|       User Training, Help Desk |
|    ⊞ Project Closure |

# Finishing off the project and closure

It is critical that the action points of the project are resolved as quickly as possible. Action points may be to revisit some areas, to extend in certain areas, or to address issues which presented themselves that were not thought of. Usually this happens when the process that users actually follow is different from the design discussions, or when what users say and do are practically different, either due to their point of reference being a legacy system, or out of pure habit. Any issues with a business process must be resolved in the system and users must agree to the new process even if it is amended after go-live for some reason.

# Change management of production environments

A well thought through and practical change management process must be implemented after go-live to ensure that the risk of breaking the business process and operation is mitigated and managed. A typical Compiere environment infrastructure after go live is as follows:

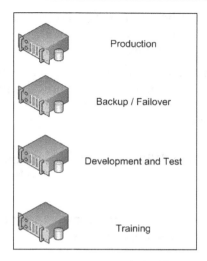

**Production server(s)**: This is the main transactional processing environment.

**Backup/Failover server(s)**: Should the production server fail, this environment would be a copy of production server. In larger environments the costs of downtime could out-weigh the cost of a proper backup/failover server environment.

**Development and Test server(s)**: This environment is where deployment files are deployed for testing by users, prior to loading onto the production server.

**Training system**: The training server is a stable environment in which a new user can be trained and gets to know the system prior to actually using it in the production environments.

# Supplier Service Level Agreement (SLA) management

The critical part in the production environment is what aspects are maintained in-house and what is expected from external parties. Some areas to consider in the management of the environments are as follows:

- **Down time and vendor response times**: How critical is the down time and how are responsibilities contractually disseminated between infrastructure, hardware, and Compiere vendors?

- **Fault reporting and follow-up**: How will issues and bugs be managed, and who will take responsibility for these aspects? How will users report issues internally, and what types of problems and resolution actions will external vendors be responsible for?

- **Monitoring aspects**: Who will manage the monitoring systems, log files, system issue reports and errors, and follow these up and report in a timely manner to management and external vendors for their response?

- **Strategic direction and enhancements**: What aspects of the system are being improved upon internally, and how are these being managed against a timeline and goals of efficiency improvement and automation? Who, internally, will be responsible for managing this aspect, or will this be outsourced?

- **New version migration**: With new versions of Compiere being released every six months, how will the implementation be migrated to new versions, and what planning is required to do this?

Some issues that the Compiere Partner and Consona Corporation. would incorporate into their SLA and Annual License are as follows:

|  | Compiere Authorized Partner | Consona Corporation |
|---|---|---|
| Pre-Sales Support | Yes | Yes |
| Implementation | Yes | Not Applicable |
| Enhancement / Customization | Yes | Product Roadmap |
| Access to Support, Documentation, Issue Tracking | First Line and Second Line Support | Product General Support |
| Support requests, Response Time support, Phone Support | Yes — Client instance related | Yes — Product General for Professional and Enterprise Editions only. |
| Source code | Commercial access | Commercial access |
| Upgrades and Service Packs | Responsible for service pack implementation and migration | Released every 3-6 Months |
| Infrastructure Support | Negotiated | Not Applicable |
| User Product Training | Yes | Online training |
| Database Support | Yes | Product General Support |

# Keeping up-to-date: Compiere migration

One of the benefits of the Compiere environment is that migration to an upgraded or latest version is a relatively seamless and safe process.

# What is migration?

**Migration** is the process of moving from one version of Compiere to another version (usually the latest version). This move involves the data and application dictionary definitions, as well as the source code. In other words, it's moving from Compiere 3.1 to 3.6 or interim releases such as 3.61. What this means is that Compiere Inc. maintains and generally supports only the latest version of Compiere. The requirement is that the older versions have to migrate to the latest version for up-to-date support.

Due to the experiences of many traditional systems, there may be consensus of **Don't touch the system once it is working**. This response is due either to the fear of losing customizations or extensions or to the cost of re-writing customizations, and sadly many professional consultants would even advise against any changes to packaged software whatsoever (the boxed-in approach). As we know, because Compiere is open source, an enhancement or customization is not a self-inflicted injury and actually the more often you migrate, the more seamless the experience becomes. However, it must be added that in real life, if the migration does fail, it is purely the technical development team that did not know what they were doing and need to skill up.

# How does migration work?

The automated aspect of the migration involves the transformation of the underlying database tables, columns, IDs, and foreign keys to the next version. The process of migration is described in the Release Notes of each version of Compiere. Behind the scenes, the process can be described as follows:

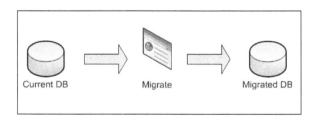

The non-automated aspect of the migration is transforming the source code from the current to the latest version, using the new version of the source code as a reference:

The migration process does not affect tenant data—it is the transformation of the underlying data structures into the latest version, and is rarely impacted. In some instances where the data is impacted, this transformation would be to accommodate more functionality, and thus the data will be transformed by the migration process, with full logs that describe the impacted aspects being created.

# Application Dictionary (AD) changes

Since the AD changes are impacted during the migration, it is important that AD changes are managed accordingly.

Dictionary versus User Maintained entity types: This relates to any non Compiere AD change, which will automatically be assigned a **User Maintained** entity type:

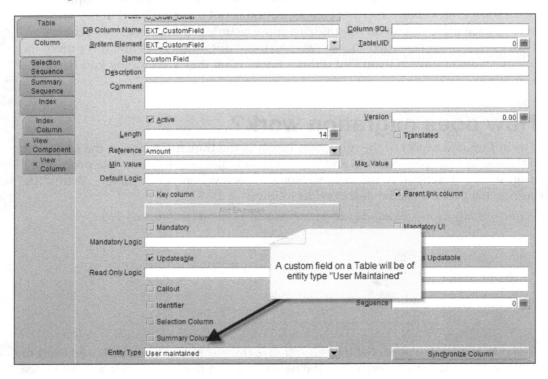

A custom field on a Table will be of entity type "User Maintained"

# Keeping AD changes after the migrate

When changing data within the AD, make sure that you assign them in the **Change Audit** menu item as a Customization change which will ensure that, as part of the migration, these custom changes can be identified and applied:

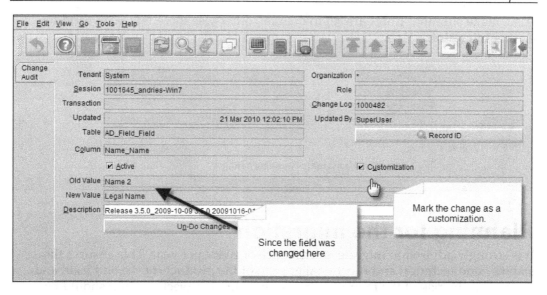

After the migration has completed, use the **Reapply Customizations** menu process in the System Administrator role:

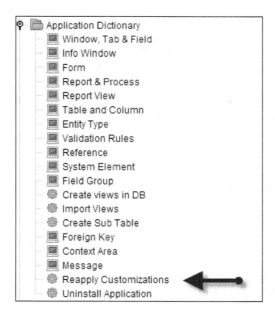

Also, make sure that **Roles** are set to manual, otherwise these will be overridden during migration:

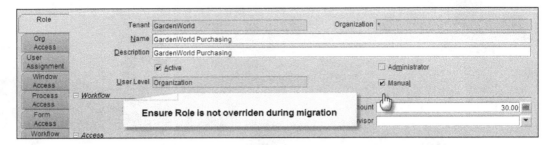

# Planning for the migration

It is strongly advised to migrate at least once or twice per year. This ensures the stability and technical and functional growth of the product for the end user, and minimizes the risk of the migration becoming a huge project, when it should be a seamless process. Thus, there are certain aspects that can be managed in order to ensure that the migration remains seamless:

- **Backup Strategy**: Ensure that the appropriate backup strategy is followed and tested.

- **Timing of Migration**: As mentioned previously, at least annual migration is advised. During an extended implementation project it is advised to migrate as regularly as possible This is to ensure that not only are the benefits of a later release enjoyed, but also that future migrations are going to be easy and that the rules have been followed.

- **Minimize and don't change the Compiere source code**: Through Java source code structuring and modeling, it is highly recommended that no direct changes to Compiere source base be made and that all code changes are made in overriding classes or custom call-outs. Compiere also allows for Component registration so as to ensure the uniqueness of applicable component entity IDs within the market place.

- **Functional migration**: Make sure to read the version's accompanying release notes for details of changes made and bugs corrected, and evaluate the impact on existing business processes. If a new module is implemented, then user training should be made within the organization's normal change management processes.

- **Database migration**: Follow up on the migration logs meticulously, and resolve items during a test migration. The test process is repeatable, and logs are very descriptive:

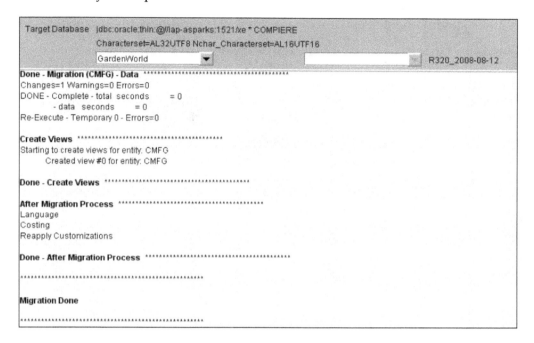

 There may be harmless messages that can be ignored; these will be identified in the release notes. Migration may sometimes require the entire process to be run twice.

# Summary

This chapter highlighted that a Compiere implementation requires the same change management process as any other major change within an organization. Due to the integrated environment, it will affect most parts of the business environment.

We explained that it is important to identify the people and ensure appropriate communication for the project. We covered an overview of technical and project requirements to reach the go-live milestone. We also listed issues to be addressed after go-live, including post-implementation support. We also covered the migration process and planning for the migration so as to ensure that the system stays up-to-date.

The success of a Compiere implementation has less to do with the actual functionality and more to do with a practical project implementation approach, and guiding management, end users, and the project role players through the implementation journey to their new environment. Any ERP system or technology is not the answer to every business problem, and although Compiere is flexible, care should be taken to implement it in a structured and phased approach, and not fall into the dreaded scope creep and code-and-fix project scenarios. Due to its designed architecture, Compiere offers large-scale enterprise scalability in its platform, as well as fast customization and a seamless and efficient migration and upgrade process.

I shout enthusiastically about Compiere because, having worked on most other major systems in the market, I have not come across a system offering the openness (it is transparent by nature), value (TCO, ROI, yes!), well thought-out design (very structured, yet flexible, thanks to Mr Jorg Janke!) and yet so fundamentally integrated in its ERP core. Happy trading!

# Index

gallons, setting up  41
litres, setting up  41
**unposted documents  142**
**user**
creating  43, 44

# V

**vendor payments**
about  114
batch processing  114-116
manual payment, selecting  117

# W

**warehouse overview  85**
**web launch, Compiere  23, 24**
**window fields, Application dictionary  160**
**window tabs, Application dictionary  160**
**window types, Application dictionary**
about  159
maintain  159
query only  159
transaction  159

## Thank you for buying
## Compiere 3

# About Packt Publishing

Packt, pronounced 'packed', published its first book "*Mastering phpMyAdmin for Effective MySQL Management*" in April 2004 and subsequently continued to specialize in publishing highly focused books on specific technologies and solutions.

Our books and publications share the experiences of your fellow IT professionals in adapting and customizing today's systems, applications, and frameworks. Our solution based books give you the knowledge and power to customize the software and technologies you're using to get the job done. Packt books are more specific and less general than the IT books you have seen in the past. Our unique business model allows us to bring you more focused information, giving you more of what you need to know, and less of what you don't.

Packt is a modern, yet unique publishing company, which focuses on producing quality, cutting-edge books for communities of developers, administrators, and newbies alike. For more information, please visit our website: www.packtpub.com.

# About Packt Open Source

In 2010, Packt launched two new brands, Packt Open Source and Packt Enterprise, in order to continue its focus on specialization. This book is part of the Packt Open Source brand, home to books published on software built around Open Source licences, and offering information to anybody from advanced developers to budding web designers. The Open Source brand also runs Packt's Open Source Royalty Scheme, by which Packt gives a royalty to each Open Source project about whose software a book is sold.

# Writing for Packt

We welcome all inquiries from people who are interested in authoring. Book proposals should be sent to author@packtpub.com. If your book idea is still at an early stage and you would like to discuss it first before writing a formal book proposal, contact us; one of our commissioning editors will get in touch with you.

We're not just looking for published authors; if you have strong technical skills but no writing experience, our experienced editors can help you develop a writing career, or simply get some additional reward for your expertise.

## SAP Business ONE Implementation

ISBN: 978-1-847196-38-5          Paperback: 320 pages

Bring the power of SAP Enterprise Resource Planning to your small-midsize business

1.  Get SAP B1 up and running quickly, optimize your business, inventory, and manage your warehouse

2.  Understand how to run reports and take advantage of real-time information

3.  Complete an express implementation from start to finish

## ADempiere 3.4 ERP Solutions

ISBN: 978-1-847197-26-9          Paperback: 460 pages

Design, configure, and implement a robust enterprise resource planning system in your organization using ADempiere

1.  Successfully implement ADempiere—an open source, company-wide ERP solution— to manage and coordinate all the resources, information, and functions of a business

2.  Master data management and centralize the functions of various business departments in an advanced ERP system

3.  Efficiently manage business documents such as purchase/sales orders, material receipts/ shipments, and invoices

4.  Extend and customize ADempiere to meet your business needs

Please check **www.PacktPub.com** for information on our titles

## Implementing Microsoft Dynamics NAV 2009

ISBN: 978-1-847195-82-1          Paperback: 552 pages

Explore the new features of Microsoft Dynamics NAV 2009, and implement the solution your business needs

1.  First book to show you how to implement Microsoft Dynamics NAV 2009 in your business

2.  Meet the new features in Dynamics NAV 2009 that give your business the flexibility to adapt to new opportunities and growth

3.  Easy-to-read style, packed with hard-won practical advice

## Apache OFBiz Development: The Beginner's Tutorial

ISBN: 978-1-847194-00-8          Paperback: 472 pages

Using Services, Entities, and Widgets to build custom ERP and CRM systems

1.  Understand how OFBiz is put together

2.  Learn to create and customize business applications with OFBiz

3.  Gain valuable development and performance hints

4.  A fully illustrated tutorial with functional step-by-step examples

Please check **www.PacktPub.com** for information on our titles

www.ingramcontent.com/pod-product-compliance
Lightning Source LLC
Chambersburg PA
CBHW060552060326
40690CB00017B/3689